BICYCLING®

MAGAZINE'S

ULTIMATE ride guide

for Road and Mountain Biking

Breakthrough Training Programs, Daily Logs, and Performance Secrets from the Pros

Rodale Press, Inc.
Emmaus, Pennsylvania

Notice

The information in this book is meant to supplement, not replace, proper cycling training. Like any sport involving speed, equipment, balance, and environmental factors, cycling poses some inherent risk. The editors and publisher advise readers to take full responsibility for their safety and know their limits. Before practicing the skills and techniques described in this book, be sure that your equipment is well-maintained, and do not take risks beyond your level of experience, aptitude, training, and comfort level.

Library of Congress Cataloging-in-Publication Data

Bicycling magazine's ultimate ride guide for road and mountain biking : breakthrough training programs, daily logs, and performance secrets from the pros.

    p.   cm.

  ISBN 1–57954–056–2   paperback

  1. Cycling—Training.   2. Bicycles—Equipment and supplies.

I. Bicycling.   II. Title: Ultimate ride guide for road and mountain biking.

GV1048.B55   1999

796.6—dc21   98–45931

Distributed to the book trade by St. Martin's Press

2 4 6 8 10 9 7 5 3 1   paperback

BICYCLING
Magazine's Ultimate Ride Guide Staff

MANAGING EDITOR: Jack Croft
EDITOR: John D. Reeser
WRITERS: John S. Allen; Arnie Baker, M.D.; Susan I. Barr, Ph.D.;
Geoff Drake; Stephen C. George; James Hargett; Richard Laliberte;
Jim Langley; Fred Matheny; John Olsen; Ed Pavelka; Bill Strickland;
Julie Walsh
PERMISSIONS: Lois Guarino Hazel
COPY EDITOR: Kathryn A. Cressman
BOOK AND COVER DESIGNERS: Susan P. Eugster, Patrick Maley
COVER PHOTOGRAPHER: Robert Houser
LAYOUT DESIGNER: Keith Biery
DIGITAL IMAGING CONSULTANT: Dale Mack
ASSOCIATE ART DIRECTOR: Charles Beasley
MANUFACTURING COORDINATORS: Brenda Miller, Jodi Schaffer,
Patrick T. Smith
OFFICE MANAGER: Roberta Mulliner
OFFICE STAFF: Julie Kehs, Suzanne Lynch, Mary Lou Stephen

Rodale Health and Fitness Books
VICE PRESIDENT AND EDITORIAL DIRECTOR: Debora T. Yost
EXECUTIVE EDITOR: Neil Wertheimer
DESIGN AND PRODUCTION DIRECTOR: Michael Ward
MARKETING MANAGER: Mark Wiragh
RESEARCH MANAGER: Ann Gossy Yermish
COPY MANAGER: Lisa D. Andruscavage
PRODUCTION MANAGER: Robert V. Anderson Jr.
ASSOCIATE STUDIO MANAGER: Thomas P. Aczel
MANUFACTURING MANAGERS: Eileen F. Bauder, Mark Krahforst

Photo Credits
PAGES 3, 5: Scott Markewitz
PAGES 6, 7: Mitch Mandel/Rodale Images
PAGES 9, 10, 11: Mitch Mandel
PAGE 29: John Hamel
PAGES 35, 36, 37, 39, 40, 41, 44, 45, 46, 47, 48, 49: Mel Lindstrom

THE ULTIMATE RIDE GUIDE TRAINING LOGS AT A GLANCE

If you use a bike computer, you can record how far and the average speed you rode

The weather, mechanical problems, who you rode with, name of trails, whatever you want

How much water and food you consumed during the ride

If you participated in any activities in addition to riding

Start time or length of your ride

Sum up your whole ride with a letter grade

Sunday

date

time

mileage

average speed

course

grade your ride

road   hilly   dry

a   b   c   d   e

mountain   flat   wet

cross-training

food/water

notes: _____
_____
_____

Summary

weekly mileage

year to date

notes: _____
_____
_____
_____

You want to alternate the intensity and length of your workouts throughout the week. Long distances and speed work equate to hard workouts and should be followed by easy rides or a day off to recuperate.

Overall notes for the week: overcoming an illness, a great week, vacations

A different tip for every week of the year

The total number of miles you rode this week

A running total of your yearly mileage

A CYCLIST'S WORLD

- Total number of cyclists in the United States: **45.1 million**

- Number of bicycles sold worldwide each year: **85 million**

- Number of bicycles sold in the United States each year: **10 million**

- Of those 10 million, number sold by mass merchants: **7 million**

- Average price for a bike from a mass merchant: **$105**

- Average assembly time for each bike: **45 minutes**

- Number of frames built by John Murphy of Columbine Cycle Works each year: **35**

- Price for a typical Columbine frame: **$2,200**

- Average construction time for each Columbine frame: **70 hours**

- Year the mountain bike was invented (allegedly): **1976**

- Total number of mountain bike models: **1,383**

- First year the off-road World Championships were held: **1990**

- Maximum size (add length, height, and depth) for a checked bag on most U.S. airlines to avoid incurring a $50 handling fee each way: **62 inches**

- Charge for checking a bicycle (88 inches) on a domestic flight: **$50 each way**

- Charge for checking golf clubs (82 inches): **$0**

- Average number of years that cyclists in England live longer than drivers in that country: **Nine**

- The most common serious bike accident in San Francisco: **Collision with a car door**

CONTENTS

Nutrition

Training Logs and Charts

INTRODUCTION

Whether you're a road or mountain biker, there's one thing that we're pretty certain of: You're passionate about your sport. We've found that cyclists love the challenge of a long road ride or the thrill of a treacherous mountain ride. They'll plunk down hundreds of dollars for the right equipment and ride in all kinds of weather. And they love to record their accomplishments.

While many use logs to track progress toward a race or distance goal, most riders just want to jot down the ups and downs of the activity they love. A dog-eared log becomes a keepsake as it fills with memories of golden jaunts through autumn woods, long country rides on early summer mornings, bone-jarring runs down steep mountainsides, and crisp rides during gray winters.

Unfortunately, for most cyclists' needs, a simple log does not exist. The logs on the market target the serious trainer or racer. They're loaded with entries like "time at maximum heart rate" or "grams of carbohydrate consumed." But all of that changes with *Bicycling Magazine's Ultimate Ride Guide*. We've designed the logs with you in mind. In addition to your journeys' particulars, you can log an overall grade for your rides. Felt great on that long Sunday spin through the country? Then give it an A. Had a tough time because you weren't feeling so hot? Give it a C. And because you probably do more than just cycle, there's room to record your other physical activities.

But this is more than just a notebook to record your road and mountain biking adventures. It's also packed with a complete spectrum of advice and tips to make cycling the ultimate experience. You can read how to fix a flat in under three minutes without using tools. Or check out the best ways to stay hydrated during cycling, the coolest and most practical gear to wear on rides, which tools you must own, or how to train for a century.

We want this log to be the last thing you put down before getting on your bike and the first thing you pick up on your return. So go ahead. Dive in and read how to have even more fun on your bicycle. The memories you create will provide years of enjoyment.

John Reeser

John Reeser

Editor

Bicycling Books

PERFECT FORM:
ROAD BIKE

1. *Handlebars:* The top of your handlebar stem should be about one inch below the top of your bike saddle. As you get more experienced, you can lower the handlebars a little bit more—the lower you can go, the more aerodynamic your cycling form.

   Make sure that your handlebars are shoulder-width apart. Also, the bottom part of the handlebars should be level or pointed slightly down toward the rear wheel hub.

2. *Brakes:* Brake levers should be positioned so your wrists are straight when you grasp the levers.

3. *Top tube/stem lengths:* To make sure that your tube and stem lengths are correct, sit on the saddle and put your hands on the brake hoods (the tops of the brake levers). Look down. Can you see the hub of the front wheel? If yes, move the stem slightly forward or backward until the handlebars block your view of the hub.

4. *Saddle:* Your saddle should be level or pointed slightly up at the tip. To determine proper saddle height, pedal a few strokes. If your knees are slightly bent at the very bottom of the stroke, your height is good. Never put the saddle so high that your knees lock.

5. *Knee-over-pedal:* When your pedals are level, check your forward leg. The bony part just below your knee should be directly over the middle or axle of the forward pedal. If it's not, adjust the saddle forward or backward slightly until you get it right.

6. *Frame:* To make sure that you have the right size frame, straddle the bicycle. There should be two to three inches clearance between the top tube and your crotch. Another guide is to check your seat post.

Assuming your saddle height is correct, roughly four to five inches of the post should be visible. If you can see more than five inches of post, chances are that your bike's frame is too small.

7. **Feet:** The widest parts of your feet should be directly over the axles of the pedals. When pedaling, the angle of your feet should be natural—not flat or uncomfortably bent up. If it isn't, adjust the cleats.

8. **Crankarms:** To know the proper size crankarms for you, you'll need to know your inseam. As a rule of thumb, if your inseam is less than 29 inches, use 165-mm crankarms; from 29 to 32 inches, use 170-mm; 32 to 34, 172.5-mm; anything more than 34 inches, 175-mm.

PERFECT FORM:
MOUNTAIN BIKE

1. *Handlebar width:* An end-to-end measurement of 21 to 24 inches is common. If the bar seems too wide, it can be trimmed with a hacksaw or pipe cutter. First, though, move your controls and grips inward and take a ride to make sure that you'll like the new width. And re-member to leave a bit extra at each end if you use bar-ends. In gen-eral, the narrower the handlebar, the quicker the steering. Wider bars provide more control at slow speed.

2. *Stem:* Mountain bike stems come in a huge variety of extensions (from 60 millimeters to 150 millimeters) and rises (from –5 to +25 degrees). For good control, the stem should place the bar an inch or two below the top of the saddle. Never exceed the stem's maximum height line; the stem could break and cause a nasty crash. Choose a stem length that allows comfortably bent arms and a straight back. A longer and lower reach works for fast cruising, but a higher, closer hand position affords more control on difficult trails.

3. *Saddle height and tilt:* Seatpost lengths of 350 millimeters or more are common, so a lot can be out of the frame before the maximum extension line shows. For efficient pedaling, your knee should remain slightly bent at the bottom of the pedal stroke (the same as with a road bike). However, you may wish to lower the saddle slightly for rough terrain, enabling you to rise up so the bike can float beneath you without pounding your crotch.

4. *Frame:* Spontaneous (sometimes unwanted) get-offs are a part of riding off road. Consequently, you need lots of clearance between you and the top tube. The ideal mountain bike size is about four inches smaller than your road bike size.

   Manufacturers specify frame size in different ways. All start at the center of the crankset axle and measure along the seat tube. But

some stop at the center of the top tube, others go to its top, and a few use the top of an extended seat lug.

5. **Crankarms:** Manufacturers usually vary this with frame size. For greater leverage on steep climbs, mountain bikes typically come with crankarms 5-millimeters longer than a road bike for the same size rider.

6. **Arms:** Slightly bent arms act as shock absorbers. If you can only reach the bar with elbows straight, get a shorter stem or condition yourself to lean forward more by rotating your hips.

7. **Back:** When your top-tube/stem-length combo is correct, you should have a forward lean of about 45 degrees during normal riding.

8. **Hands and wrists:** Grasp the bar just firmly enough to maintain control. Set the brake levers close to the grips and angle them so you can extend a finger or two around each and still hold the bar comfortably. Always ride with your thumbs under the bar so your hands won't slip on a bump.

PRERIDE
STRETCHING ROUTINE

Stretching is a hard sell to most cyclists, who wonder why they need flexibility. After all, your range of motion is limited to the circumference of the crankarm's circle or the reach for a water bottle. So why should you spend precious riding time on flexibility?

You'll be more aerodynamic. If you want a low, aero position on a road or time-trial bike, flexibility is crucial. *Bicycling* magazine fitness advisory board member Andrew Pruitt, Ed.D., says you can't get truly aero if you can't touch your toes—cold, with no warmup—without bending your knees.

You'll suffer fewer injuries. A little limberness helps in a crash. When you auger in, you're going to need a lot of looseness in a hurry. "If you fall in an awkward position, flexibility will help you avoid injury," says Bob Anderson, author of the bestseller *Stretching*.

You'll enjoy the rest of your life. "Even if you're obsessed, you still do more than ride," says Anderson. "If you run, play other sports, or just sit at a desk all day, stretching protects you from injury and dissipates tension."

You'll age with grace. "Stretching helps as your muscles stiffen with age. You don't have the same flexibility you did when you were 25. The goal is to be as flexible in 20 years as you are now," says Anderson.

Here are four preride stretches that Anderson recommends for cyclists—and you can use your bike as a prop while doing them. *Safety alert:* If you're wearing slick-soled road shoes, do these stretches on grass or another nonslip surface.

Back and Shoulders

Place your feet about four feet from the bike and bend 90 degrees at the waist. Put one hand on the saddle, the other on the handlebar. Relax; keep your arms straight and your feet directly under your hips. Bend your knees slightly. Slowly move your chest down until you feel a gentle stretch in your arms, shoulders, and back. Hold for 15 seconds, relax, and repeat. When you come out of this stretch, save strain on your back muscles by bending your knees more before standing.

Calves

To stretch your right calf, stand three feet from your bike and lean on it with your right forearm on the saddle and your left hand on the handlebar. Step forward with your left leg, bending your knee. Keep your right knee straight behind you with your right foot about 18 inches behind the left. Slowly move your hips forward until you feel a stretch in your right calf. Keep the heel of your right foot on the ground and your toes pointed straight ahead. Hold an easy stretch for 15 seconds, relax, and repeat. Then stretch your left calf.

Quads

Stand next to your bike and hold the saddle with your right hand. With your left hand, grasp your right foot behind you and pull it up gently across your buttocks. Stretch your quads gently for 15 seconds, relax, and repeat. Do both legs. Your knee bends at a natural angle when you grab your foot with the opposite hand, so this stretch is good for problem knees.

Hamstrings

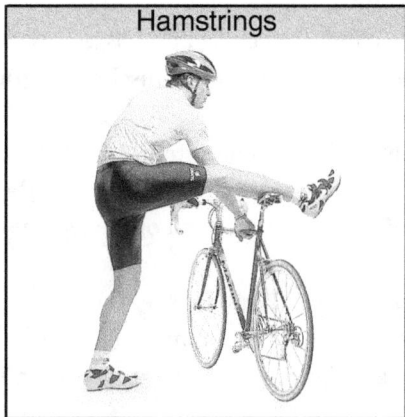

Lift your right leg and place the middle of your calf on the saddle. Steady the bike with your left hand on the handlebar and your right on the top tube. Your right knee should be bent about an inch. Your left knee should be slightly flexed with your foot pointing straight ahead in a walking position. Slowly bend from the waist, eyes forward, until you feel a mild stretch in the back of your right leg. Hold for 15 seconds, relax, and repeat. Then stretch your left hamstring.

STRENGTH TRAINING
FOR CYCLISTS

Whether you're a road cyclist or a mountain biker, your workout is going to be pretty much the same.

"Cycling is universally hard on the legs and lower back. But because you're using your upper body to steer and help control the bike, you'll also want to pay attention to muscles there—that's something a lot of cyclists forget," says John Graham, director of the Human Performance Center at the Allentown Sports Medicine and Human Performance Center in Pennsylvania.

The routine starting on the opposite page should help you keep a proper fitness balance between your upper and lower body, while providing the benefit of targeting the following cycling muscles, says Graham.

Arms. Whether you're bumping down a long, rough mountain or tugging on those handlebars as you climb a steep hill in the road, you're going to need strong arms to handle the job. "Barbell and dumbbell curls will strengthen the biceps, but don't forget the triceps for muscle balance and stabilization," Graham says. He recommends overhead triceps extensions. Also do wrist and forearm exercises, such as wrist curls and reverse wrist curls, to give you plenty of strength and endurance to keep the bike stable.

Upper back. Along with your arms, your upper back is going to help you pull up on the handlebars when you're climbing; it also absorbs plenty of shock during a ride. One-arm dumbbell rows will enhance muscle strength and endurance for the upper back.

Legs. Yeah, you'd think pedaling over hill and dale would be exercise enough for the legs. Don't believe it, says Graham. "Cycling really works the quads and the muscles on the outsides of the thighs. The rest of the leg muscles don't get as much benefit."

Focus on building well-rounded leg strength. Perform squats to ensure proper balance between the quadriceps and opposing hamstring muscles. Also, to strengthen your inner- and outer-thigh muscles, do abductor and adductor lifts.

Barbell Curl

Stand and grab a barbell so your palms are facing up; your hands should be about shoulder-width apart. In the starting position, your arms should be extended so the barbell will be at about thigh level. With your back straight and your elbows close to your sides, lift the barbell, curling it up toward your collarbone. Lower the barbell back to the starting position. That's one rep; do as many as you can. Keep your wrists straight and do the curls slowly.

Overhead Triceps Extension

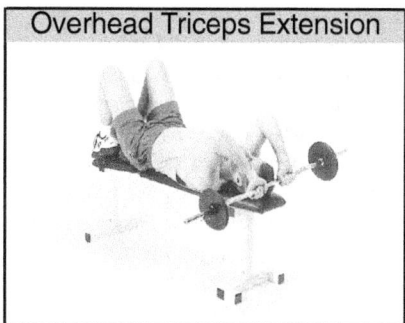

Lie on your back on a weight bench. Make sure that your back is in full contact with the bench. If your lower back arches when your feet are on the floor, pull your feet up to the end of the bench. Hold a barbell above your chest, arms extended. Your hands should be only four to six inches apart, palms facing away from you. Slowly lower the weight toward the top of your head, bending your arms at the elbows. Remember to keep your elbows pointed toward the ceiling and shoulder-width apart. If you have trouble doing that, the weight is probably too heavy. Extend your arms back out to the starting position, then repeat for as many reps as you can.

Bench Press

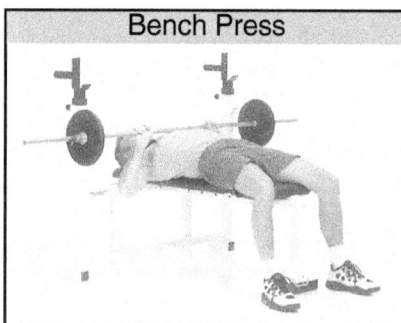

Lie on a weight bench. Grasp a barbell above your chest with a medium grip (hands about shoulder-width apart) or a slightly wider grip. Your palms should face your legs, and your feet should rest flat on the ground. Keep your back straight and against the bench. Lower the barbell to your chest, right at nipple level. Your elbows should be pointed out while the rest of your body remains in position. Don't arch your back or bounce the bar off your chest. Raise to the starting position and repeat to exhaustion.

One-Arm Dumbbell Row

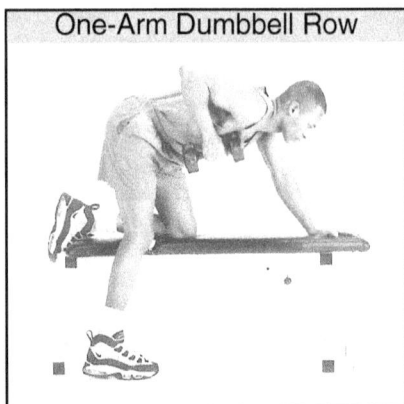

Stand partly over a weight bench, with your body weight resting on your bent left leg and left hand, both of which should be on the center of the padded portion of the bench. With your right foot firmly on the floor, hold a dumbbell in your right hand. Keep your back straight; your eyes should be facing the ground. Extend your right arm down toward the ground, elbow unlocked. Pull the weight up and in toward your torso. Raise it as high as you can, bringing it in to your lower-chest muscles. Your right elbow should be pointing up toward the ceiling as you lift. Repeat to muscle exhaustion. This exercise works the back without much risk of throwing it out. Although it seems like your arm is doing all the work, don't over-compensate and try to get more of your back behind the lift. You'll likely injure yourself.

Alternating Press with Dumbbells

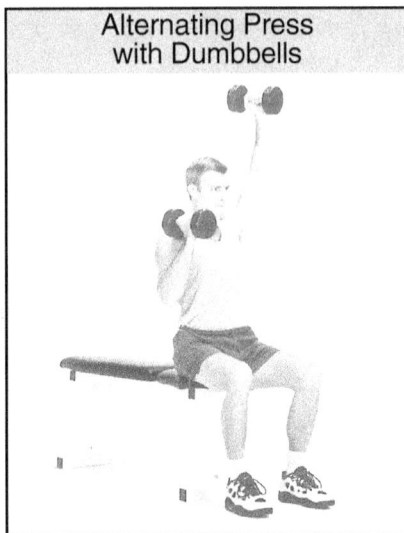

Do this while sitting on a weight bench. Grasping two dumbbells, sit on the end of a bench with your legs slightly parted. Your feet should be firmly on the floor, your forearms raised. Keep the dumbbells shoulder-width apart, at shoulder level, with your palms facing each other. Keep your shoulders back, your chest out, and a slight forward lean in your lower back. Keep your elbows unlocked. Raise the left dumbbell up until your arm is straight, but don't lock your elbow. Lower, then repeat with the other arm. Repeat, alternating your repetitions, until you reach muscle exhaustion.

Wrist Curl

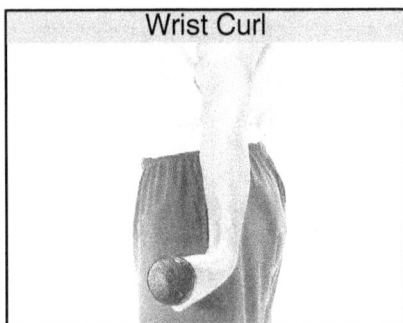

Hold a comfortable weight (five pounds or less) at your side. With your elbow locked and your palm facing forward, roll your wrist as far forward as it will go comfortably, and then let it back down slowly. Repeat to muscle exhaustion.

Reverse Wrist Curl

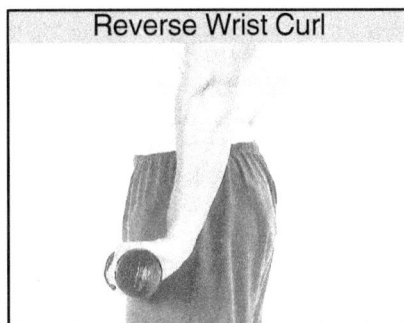

Same as the wrist curl, except your palm faces backward. Flex your wrist forward as far as it will go comfortably, then let it down. Repeat to muscle exhaustion.

Crunch

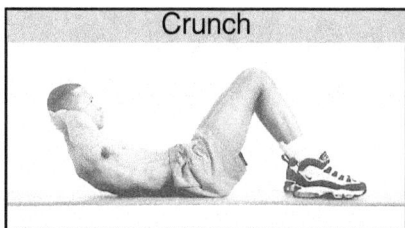

Lie flat on your back with your hands cupped near your ears or crossed over your chest—never pull on your neck during a crunch, because you could end up injuring your neck or upper back. Keep your feet together, flat on the floor and about six inches from your buttocks. Bend your knees at about a 45-degree angle, and keep your legs slightly apart. Curl your upper torso up and in toward your knees until your shoulder blades are as high off the ground as you can get them. Only your shoulders should lift, not your lower back. Feel your abs contract, and hold the raise for a second. Lower to the starting position, then continue with your next rep without relaxing in between. Continue reps until muscle exhaustion. As your abs get stronger, you can hold a light weight plate across your chest and do your crunches that way.

Squat

This barbell exercise works not only the quads but also the hamstrings, the muscles on the backs of your thighs. Hold a barbell with your palms facing forward and place it behind your neck—it should be even across your upper shoulder muscles. Stand up straight with your feet hip-width apart, toes forward and slightly out. Bend your knees slightly, and lean slightly forward. Now squat down as though you're about to sit in a chair. Your thighs should be parallel to the floor. Go any lower and you risk injuring your knees—or falling on your butt. Keep your feet flat. Rise to the starting position, then repeat to exhaustion.

Abductor Lift

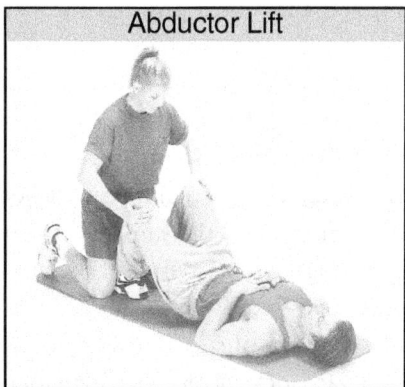

To work the outer-thigh muscles, lie on your back on the floor. Bend your legs and place your feet flat on the floor, knees together. Have your partner kneel opposite you, with her hands on the outside of your knees. Try to spread your legs, pushing your knees apart. While you do this, your partner should apply inward pressure. Hold for a count of 12, then relax briefly and repeat. Do 8 to 12 reps.

Adductor Lift

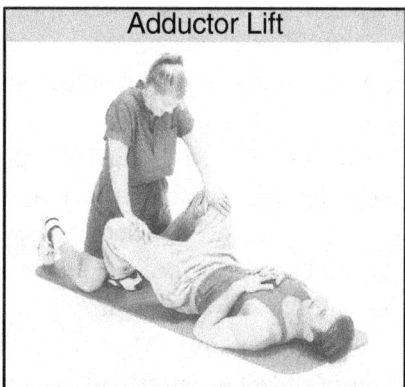

For your inner-thigh muscles, assume the abductor-lift position, but this time, put the soles of your feet together, knees pointing outward. Your partner should apply pressure to the insides of your knees while you try to bring your legs together. Hold for a count of 12, then relax briefly and repeat. Do 8 to 12 reps.

BETTER TRAINING
FOR MOUNTAIN BIKERS

For years, road riders have been poked, prodded, and bled in the name of science. But only recently have the folks in white coats started to make mountain bikers squirm around in the petri dish of athletic performance. The results of one important study may change the way you train.

The study was conducted at the Olympic Training Center in Colorado Springs, Colorado, by researchers Sharon McDowell, Ph.D., Edmund Burke, Ph.D., and Rebecca Milot-Bradford. "The goal of the study," says Dr. McDowell, "was to see whether cycling abilities measured in the lab carry over to performance in the real world of racing."

To find out, the subjects—14 male expert-level mountain bikers—performed a series of lab tests carefully designed to measure four important cycling attributes: power at lactate threshold, anaerobic power, technique, and strength. To determine the intensity level that can be sustained in a steady effort (power at lactate threshold), subjects labored through an ergometer test that revealed how much power they could produce for long periods of time. To check how quickly power tailed off due to fatigue (for instance, how you might feel riding hard over a series of short hills), riders hammered five consecutive all-out 30-second efforts with minimal rest between each sprint (anaerobic power). Researchers also measured bike-handling skills by timing the subjects in a section of an actual race, followed by a time trial over difficult terrain. This determined the impact of technique. Finally, to measure upper-body strength, the riders did as many bench rows as possible using 35 percent of their body weight.

According to Dr. McDowell, the measurement of steady power output (power at lactate threshold) was the best yardstick of race performance. "That was significantly related to performance for all three races used for comparison. The anaerobic data, repeated 30-second sprints, were less clearly related but were significant for one race that included lots of hard climbing and gnarly descending."

Technique also correlated to all three race performances. Upper-body strength only showed a correlation in the final race of the season. Dr. Mc-Dowell speculates that this may be an indication that over the course of a long season, overall body strength becomes more important.

Dr. McDowell analyzed each subject's training diary to see how the intensity and number of workouts correlated with race results. In general, "the better riders had a lot more structure in their training than the slower ones had," she says. "If you're new to the sport, it helps to get a coach to show you how to set up your season plan and get the most from your time on the bike."

If you don't have a coach, here are some workouts Dr. McDowell suggests.

Crank up the power. Off-road races are a bit like road time trials where pack tactics don't count—you just go as hard as you can for the distance. Assuming you have a good fitness base, these three workouts will increase the power you can produce during efforts of 30 minutes to an hour. They can be done on a mountain bike on smooth terrain (such as fire roads) or on a road bike. Warm up for at least 20 minutes first.

1. Ride hard for 15 minutes at an intensity that you can barely maintain for the distance. Spin easily for 10 minutes to recover. Increase by one repeat each week until you reach three.

2. Find a long, moderate hill that takes about 30 minutes to climb. Climb it twice a week at a steady, hard pace. If there are no long hills nearby, ride hard for 30 minutes on a flat road, into the wind.

3. Ride a local time trial once a week. There's no substitute for competition to make you work hard. Don't have a road bike? Ride your mountain bike.

Increase your pain threshold (anaerobic tolerance). Once you've built steady-state power, says Dr. McDowell, work on your ability to survive repeated hard bursts. After a warmup, do three 30-second intervals with a minute rest between each one. Pedal easily for 10 minutes, then do another set of three intervals. As your recovery improves, increase each effort to one minute. Do these on flats as well as on hills.

Get technical. The message is clear: "You need to spend significant time on technical trails," says Dr. McDowell. "Ride and reride tough sections. Get coaching to help you improve your skills. Consider videotaping these practice sessions for later analysis. Train with better riders and follow their lines."

PEDAL LIKE THE PROS

How can you develop a mercury-smooth pedaling style? A stroke so smooth that others can barely tell you're pedaling at all? To find out, we talked to Craig Griffin, U.S. national endurance track coach, the man in charge of teaching trackies to go 30 mph at supersonic pedaling cadences of 120 to 140 rpm. Because they hit those revs on fixed gears (no coasting), trackies had better be smooth, or they'll bounce all over their saddles.

For Griffin, smooth pedaling, even on a bike with a conventional drive-train, is the secret to compensating for any lack of talent a rider might have. "Genetics determine how fast you can ride, but good pedal mechanics let you make the most of your gifts. If you can sit comfortably in the saddle at high rpm, you won't fade at the end of the ride—whether it's a 4,000-meter pursuit or a century. And you can use a lower gear and a higher rpm if you have the right technique, saving your legs for when it really counts." Here's how you can be mistaken for a pro.

Bring down your saddle. You're less likely to bounce when pedaling fast if you lower your saddle 2 to 3 mm compared to normal. (The standard slightly higher recommendation is to have your heel just graze the pedal when the pedal is at the bottom and your leg is allowed to hang freely.) Also, consider using shorter crankarms to reduce the diameter of the pedaling circle. This will decrease your footspeed at a given rpm. Although it's often thought that taller riders should use longer crankarms, Griffin notes that top U.S. sprinter and Olympic medalist Marty Nothstein, who is six foot two, uses relatively short (167.5 mm) crankarms so he can spin faster.

Pedal all the way around. When you've pushed down on the pedal, your leg's job isn't done. Focus on pulling through with your hamstring at the bottom of the stroke, then rolling your knee up and forward to get the pedal through "top dead-center." This is known in cycling as pedaling circles, and it's easier to practice this technique at a slightly slower cadence. Incorporate pedaling drills into your rides twice a week.

Go spinning. To work on increasing your pedal speed, get a cyclecomputer with a cadence counter. "When national team riders come to the Olympic Training Center for the first time, we issue these right away so they can learn what the correct cadence feels like," says Griffin. "It provides immediate feedback." (Most road riders should strive for a cadence of 80 to 100 rpm.)

"Your heart rate will increase when you spin," says Griffin, "so we do our intervals in a smaller gear at a very high rpm. Because our riders aren't muscling a big gear and killing their legs, they can do more repeats. Soon, a training adaptation takes place, and they can pedal a given speed at a lower heart rate."

After a few weeks of working on your spin, you should be able to determine your optimum cadence. Do some 10-minute time trials at the same speed but in different gears, and check your heart rate. Find out where you're most economical (lowest heart rate for a given cadence). Then use these exercises to expand your range.

Try training rollers. If your pedal stroke stays stubbornly ragged, consider riding a fixed-gear bike on rollers. "If you spin too fast and start bouncing in the saddle, you'll bounce right off the rollers—and that's useful feedback," says Griffin.

Another trick: Put two pieces of tape on the front roller about six inches apart, and try to keep the front wheel between them. As you get better, decrease the distance between the tape strips. (Check with your local bike shop to learn how to set up a fixed-gear bike.)

Stay in the saddle. Practice pedaling down a long, gradual hill in a low gear (for example, 42 × 17) as fast as possible with bouncing in the saddle.

Proper pedaling technique will improve your performance and help keep you injury-free, so it's important to spend some time making sure that you're doing it right. Try these tips and pretty soon you'll be mistaken for a pro.

MORE SKILL
AND SPEED RIGHT NOW

There's no denying the effectiveness of training plans and season-long goals. But wouldn't it be nice if you could become a better cyclist this afternoon, even if the improvement was only a tiny one?

Here's the best advice to help you achieve this small but satisfying goal.

1. Instead of actively drawing air into your lungs and then passively letting it out, as in normal breathing, do the opposite: Actively push air out and then passively let it in. This technique not only increases airflow but also it helps you breathe evenly instead of panting.

2. Do as racers do and start a climb in a slightly lower gear than you need. Then you may be able to shift up as you near the top, passing other riders instead of being passed. This will do wonders for your confidence.

3. Thirty minutes before a two-hour ride, eat one energy bar and drink 12 to 16 ounces of water. This will top off your fuel stores and help postpone the fatiguing effects of dehydration. We guarantee you'll have one of your best rides ever.

4. If you have a wristwatch with a timer, set it to beep every 15 minutes on your next ride. This is your signal to take a slug of water. Ride with the watch for a week, until drinking at regular intervals becomes second nature. Dehydration is the most preventable cause of cycling fatigue.

5. Increase your stability during road descents by pedaling instead of coasting. Staying in a high gear will also allow you to accelerate if the situation calls for sudden speed. Off road, shift to the middle or big ring for descents, to keep the chain from derailing.

6. To keep from skidding during off-road descents, apply the front brake firmly. There's more weight on the front tire, so you can main-

tain more control. Just make sure to stay low and back on the saddle to keep from flipping forward. Also be careful on curves, where front braking can cause a sideways wipeout.

7. Shift 20 percent more often. With the advent of index shifting and convenient handlebar-mounted levers, changing gears is easier than ever. But most road riders still don't do enough of it. To be as efficient an engine as possible and minimize knee strain, keep your pedal rpm in the 80 to 100 range. (To calculate this, count how many times your right foot reaches the bottom of the pedal stroke in 15 seconds, then multiply by four.)

8. Adjust your mountain bike's tire pressure because you're probably riding with too much off road. Excess air reduces traction and the cushioning ability of fat tires. You can usually gain more control by riding inflations of 30 to 35 psi. (Adjust to your weight, riding style, and surface conditions. Too little pressure in rough terrain can result in pinch or "snakebite" punctures.)

9. Keep your elbows bent throughout the ride. Many cyclists begin with the proper posture, but slip out of position as they fatigue. This tires you even more. To prevent this, check yourself by looking at your shadow or your reflection in passing windows, or ask your riding partner to keep an eye on your form.

10. Look for tell-tale changes in ground color when cycling off road. In dry climates, for instance, darker soil usually harbors more moisture and better traction.

11. To power over obstacles, loose ground, and other off-road debris, use the strength of your upper body to dynamically pulse the rear tire. Do this by standing, bending your elbows, lowering your head toward the stem, and pulling back and up on the handlebar at the beginning of each pedal stroke. It's sort of a seesaw rowing action that switches on your power.

12. To pick up an extra mile per hour (or more), tell yourself to pedal "faster" instead of "harder." The former helps quicken your pedal cadence, while the latter tends to tense your muscles and increase your mental strain.

FIXES FOR ACHES AND PAINS

y legs hurt. I have a cold. I'm recovering from an injury. How often have you heard (or used) these excuses as a way to say, "I don't feel like riding." Sure, pain is our bodies' distress signal, but thanks to an army of sports doctors, it's increasingly easier to heal or even eliminate the most common ailments in cycling. Here, Arnie Baker, M.D., *Bicycling* magazine's fitness advisory board member, cycling coach, and multiple U.S. national champion, pinpoints the most common cyclist aches and pains—and suggests quick fixes that'll get you back in the saddle.

You have a stuffy nose. Whether or not to ride with a cold or respiratory infection is usually an individual decision. Most of the time, there is little recourse except to take it easy and perhaps use a comfort medication like acetaminophen, aspirin, or decongestants. Sometimes you feel up to an easy spin, sometimes you want to be in bed. But stay off the bike if you're experiencing any of the following three conditions: a fever, coughing up green or yellow discharge, or a cold in your chest rather than in your nose.

You hack up your lungs after a hard ride. Coughing, not wheezing, is the most common symptom of both asthma and exercise-induced bronchospasm. Nearly everyone coughs after a hard ride on the bike, but frequent coughing may indicate a constriction of your bronchial tubes. As many as one-third of elite-level cyclists have this problem, but doctors sometimes miss the diagnosis because the chest sounds clear through the stethoscope, and routine screening tests don't always reveal it. Once the problem is identified, treatment options are numerous.

You get numb down there. A numb penis is one of the most frequent personal problems a male cyclist encounters. Sensation usually returns relatively quickly after getting off the bike. Pressure to the pudendal nerve or its blood supply is to blame. Riding in the drops or on low aero bars worsens the problem, while changing to a more upright riding position or a different saddle often improves it. Don't ignore this problem, because it could lead to permanent nerve dysfunction.

Your knees ache. Although cycling often helps knee problems, overuse injuries can still occur. A few simple rules of thumb: If the pain is in the front of your knee, raise your saddle several millimeters. If it's in the back, lower your saddle. If the pain is on the side of your knee, reposition your cleat to point your toe a little more in the direction of the pain.

Your road rash looks like raw hamburger. Sure, scrub out the dirt after a fall. But don't stop there. The secret to quick healing is to keep scabs from forming, because they block oxygen from reaching the wound. Healing is often twice as fast, with much less scarring and pain, if you cover wounds for about 10 days. After a thorough scrubbing, smear on a layer of antibiotic cream or ointment. Then apply a nonstick gauze dressing. Follow with regular gauze held in place with tape or a conforming mesh. Reapply the ointment each time you change the dressing—about once or twice a day.

Riding has become a pain in the neck. A weak neck is a strained neck. Allow for a gradual increase in endurance riding—about 10 percent a week. Consciously relax your upper body every few minutes. Look around. Use a lightweight helmet. Raise and shorten your stem to allow a more upright position. Grasp the brake lever hoods or the tops of the bars—don't ride in the drops.

Your hands feel tingly. Prevent jarring and carpal tunnel syndrome by using padded gloves and padded handlebar tape. Front suspension often helps, too. Move your hands around on the bar frequently. Raising your stem height, using a shorter stem, and moving the saddle back all help take pressure off your hands. Finally, avoid placing weight on the problem wrist by using that hand to drink from your water bottle.

Your leg muscles just seized up. Cramps can be agonizing—sudden seizing of the muscles just when you want to ride hard. No one knows for certain why cramps occur in certain individuals. Likely causes include heat, humidity, and insufficient training. If you are going to ride a century, prepare with long rides of up to 75 miles. Competitors: Races have jumps and surges, so train with intervals and sprints. Also, replace fluids and electrolytes as you ride. Consider an on-the-back hydration system for long rides, and ingest adequate fluid during the 24 hours before the event.

TRAIN FOR A CENTURY

Despite the fact that a century ride sounds impossible to some riders, each year, thousands of cyclists accomplish the feat. For those who are unprepared, the challenge of a century comes not from the miles or the terrain but from trying to coax a poorly nourished or undertrained body past its limits. With focus, you can face 100 miles being fit, rested, and well-fed. This doesn't mean the ride will be simple or too easy. The distance will still be a challenge, but you'll have given yourself a fair chance. You'll be more likely to swap success stories instead of excuses at the finish.

Goal 1 is for a cyclist who is attempting his first century and who has been averaging 45 to 50 miles per week or less. If you've been riding more, increase the recommended distances slightly or jump to the tougher program.

Goal 1: To Ride 100 Miles

Week	Mon.	Tues.	Wed.	Thurs.	Fri.	Sat.	Sun.	Weekly Mileage
	Easy	Pace	Brisk		Pace	Pace	Pace	
1	6	10	12	Off	10	30	9	77
2	7	11	13	Off	11	34	10	86
3	8	13	15	Off	13	38	11	98
4	8	14	17	Off	14	42	13	108
5	9	15	19	Off	15	47	14	119
6	11	15	21	Off	15	53	16	131
7	12	15	24	Off	15	59	18	143
8	13	15	25	Off	15	65	20	153
9	15	15	25	Off	15	65	20	155
Event Week	15	15	25	Off	10	5 Easy	Event	170

Follow Goal 2 if your weekly mileage is higher than 75. This schedule will help you finish the century with strength to spare. It can also be used by century veterans to train for a personal record. In both charts, "easy" means a leisurely ride, "pace" means matching the speed you want to maintain during the century, and "brisk" means riding faster than your century speed. If your century is on a Saturday, move the final week's training back one day.

Goal 2: A Century with Strength to Spare

Week	Mon.	Tues.	Wed.	Thurs.	Fri.	Sat.	Sun.	Weekly Mileage
	Easy	Pace	Brisk		Pace	Pace	Pace		
1	10	12	14	Off	12	40	15	103
2	10	13	13	Off	13	44	17	112
3	10	15	17	Off	15	48	18	123
4	11	16	19	Off	16	53	20	135
5	12	18	20	Off	18	59	22	149
6	13	19	23	Off	19	64	24	162
7	14	20	25	Off	20	71	27	177
8	16	20	27	Off	20	75	29	187
9	17	20	30	Off	20	75	32	194
Event Week	19	20	30	Off	10	5 Easy	Event	184

TRAIN FOR A DOUBLE CENTURY

e asked some of the country's best double-century riders this question: What advice would you give a recreational century rider who wants to try a double? Here are their answers.

Use the century as a guide. If you can finish a moderate century in eight hours and not be dead, you can do a double. The step up is not that great. In fact, progressing from 25 to 75 miles is harder. If your legs, buttocks, and hands can take 100 miles, they can take 200.

Go long. Do consecutive long rides (80 to 100 miles each day) on several weekends in addition to regular weekday training. Also plan at least one ride of 120 to 130 miles for experience and confidence.

Choose carefully. Pick a double that has a good reputation for support, but don't fall prey to the hospitality. Keep stops short, about 5 to 10 minutes, which will reduce the time you might have to ride after sundown. Eat, drink, and keep moving.

Ride with a friend. Don't do your first double alone. When you're with others, it makes the whole ride seem quicker and more fun.

Fill up. It's very important to drink a lot and to start right away. The biggest mistake people make is going out hard and neglecting to drink. Maybe you can get away with that in a century, but not in a double.

Take along "easy" food. Eat things that are easy to chew, swallow, and digest. Try things like bananas, oranges, and sweet treats you can pick up at rest stops and take with you.

Take some Tums. Not for an upset stomach, but to ward off leg cramps. They're rich in calcium and they're absorbed fast. At the first sign of a cramp, just chew a couple.

Shun hills. Pick a relatively flat first double to help ensure a positive experience.

Pace yourself. A big problem is people who go with the lead pack and jam in the fast paceline. It's fun, the endorphins are flowing—and they're cooked in 70 miles. Then the next 130 are torture. The key is to pace your-self and avoid any paceline that is above your ability.

"Easy" means a leisurely ride, "pace" means matching the speed you want to maintain during the double century, and "brisk" means riding faster than your double-century speed. Most double centuries begin on a Saturday. If yours does, take an easy ride the next day, unless your double century extends into Sunday. If your double century begins on a Sunday, ride 13 easy on Saturday.

Double-Century Training Program

Week	Mon.	Tues.	Wed.	Thurs.	Fri.	Sat.	Sun.	Weekly Mileage
	Easy	Pace	Brisk		Pace	Pace	Pace	
1	10	12	14	Off	12	40	15	103
2	10	13	15	Off	13	44	17	112
3	10	15	17	Off	15	48	18	123
4	11	16	19	Off	16	53	20	135
5	12	18	20	Off	18	59	22	149
6	13	19	23	Off	19	64	24	162
7	14	20	25	Off	20	71	27	177
8	16	20	27	Off	20	75	29	187
9	17	20	30	Off	20	75	32	194
10	20	24	30	Off	24	83	32	213
11	23	26	33	Off	26	91	35	234
12	25	28	35	Off	28	103	38	257
13	28	31	38	Off	31	113	42	283
14	31	34	41	Off	34	124	47	311
15	34	38	45	Off	38	136	51	342
16	37	42	49	Off	42	150	56	376
Event Week	38	35	39	Off	10 Easy	Event	13 Easy	335

IMPORTANT
TRAFFIC RULES

It may sound crazy, but cyclists should try to make life easier for motorists. After all, it's in our self-interest to make the road a safer, more pleasant place. Here are some easy ways to minimize the chance of conflict. These are particularly effective for novice or casual cyclists who have yet to develop the necessary confidence, fitness, or bikehandling ability to be assertive in traffic.

Stay to the right. This most basic rule of sharing the road with motor vehicles is the one that cyclists are most casual about. If there's a wide, clean shoulder, use it. Barring potholes, storm grates, parked cars, glass, and other hazards, it's usually easier (and safer) to ride to the right. If there is no safe shoulder, ride as far to the left of the white line as it takes to prevent drivers from attempting to squeeze past and put you in danger. Just avoid being in the traffic flow for no apparent reason.

Be careful when riding abreast. It's enjoyable to ride side-by-side with a companion and carry on a conversation. But road and traffic conditions may be such that vehicles back up behind you when they could otherwise get by. Thus, restrict side-by-side riding to quiet secondary roads. Even if you're alone, traffic may back up, especially on narrow, winding roads with limited visibility. Wave vehicles to come around when the path is clear.

Try not to force vehicles to repass you. Let's say you're riding along a narrow, busy road, and motorists are having trouble getting by. There are half a dozen waiting at the next red light, all of whom have already patiently overtaken you. Do you maintain your place in line, or do you zip up the right, past everyone, so you'll get the jump when the light changes? If you do the latter, you might gain 50 feet and save a few seconds, but you'll also probably create six anti-bicyclists when they get caught behind you again.

Admittedly, the scenario becomes trickier if, by hanging back, you miss the light. There are two tactful ways around this: One is to only move up in line far enough to just make the light. The other is to ride to the light, but move out slowly and slightly to the right when it turns green, letting the cars

24

through the intersection first. One other courtesy at traffic lights: Avoid blocking drivers who want to turn right on red.

Ride predictably. This one is easy. Ride in a straight line when you're cruising, and use hand signals when turning or changing lanes. If you're riding erratically, it's difficult for drivers to know when to pass. They may let several relatively safe opportunities go by before becoming exasperated and taking a dangerous chance. Hand signals are a courtesy and an important part of safe cycling. Point with your left arm for a left turn, and your right arm for a right turn. Motorists feel more comfortable dealing with cyclists who communicate their intentions. More important, drivers tend to show them more respect.

Avoid busy roads. It's surprising how often you see cyclists on a busy highway, ruffling the delicate feathers of already edgy commuters. An alternate route doesn't have to be a residential street with stop signs every other block or a glass-littered, jogger-strewn bike path. Examine a detailed map of your area, and you'll probably be surprised at the relatively quiet roads available nearby.

Be seen. In conditions where motorists might not readily see you (an overcast day, for example), it's a courtesy and plain good sense to wear brightly colored clothes. At night, drivers who encounter cyclists riding without lights, reflectors, and light-colored clothes are right to consider them menaces.

Be careful about "provocative" actions. At a red light, even friendly drivers are likely to be irritated by a cyclist riding in circles in front of them. Similarly, if you lean on a vehicle at a stoplight, be aware that some drivers consider their cars extensions of themselves. You wouldn't want anyone leaning on your bike, would you?

Practice courteous behavior. Cyclists come to appreciate little unexpected courtesies from motorists. For instance, we all nod a thank-you to the driver who has the right-of-way but waves us through anyway. Try returning the favor. You might, for example, motion a driver to make his turn in front of you if you'll be slow getting under way. Who knows—that driver may look a bit more favorably on the next cyclist down the road.

Know how to stop. Stop behind a crosswalk if there are pedestrians, but creep over it if there aren't any. Find the visibility point (the point near the crosswalk line where you start to see pedestrians and crossing car traffic). From here to the edge of the actual traffic line, go as slow as possible, looking each way for cars. Try to keep both feet on the pedals so you can quickly get moving again. Cross the intersection as soon as you see a safe gap in the crossing traffic. If no gap appears, put a foot down and wait for one.

How to Handle Tough Traffic Situations

Let's face it—some traffic situations go beyond the normal rules. When the traffic system begins to break down because of overcrowding, poor planning, and disrespect for the law, you may have to "bushwhack" your way through the mess.

When traffic lights don't turn green. Always stop and wait at red lights. You ensure your safety and increase respect for cyclists. But some traffic lights don't turn green until they receive a signal from a metal detector buried in the pavement. A bicycle doesn't have enough metal to make many of them work.

Recognize the detector by a square or octagonal pattern of thin lines in the pavement where slots were cut for the detecting wires. The detector is most sensitive if you ride along one of the wires.

If your bike doesn't trip the detector, you have to wait for a car to do it, or else you have to go through the red light. Going through the red isn't against the law, because the light is defective. If you ever have an accident or get a traffic ticket because a traffic light won't turn green, it's the fault of whoever installed the detector.

Riding through traffic jams. Traffic jams don't have to stop you—that's one of the biggest advantages of bicycling in the city. But in the tight quarters of a tie-up, take extra care.

If there is an open passing lane, use it rather than thread between cars. If the street is completely plugged, pick your way forward slowly and with your hands on the brake levers. Remember, any car door could open.

If you're in a traffic jam, you can be fairly sure that the cars will not move, since they have nowhere to go. But if there's an open driveway or parking space into which a car could turn, you have to assume that it will. Look to see whether the car's front wheels are turned. Move away from the side of the car as you pass, and try to get the driver's attention as you approach the front of the car.

Don't pass a long truck or bus in a traffic jam unless there's an entire open lane next to it. If you ride close to the side of such a vehicle, it may begin to merge toward you, leaving you no way to escape.

As you approach an intersection, change lanes to the same position you would take in normal traffic. Before you cross in front of a car to change lanes, make eye contact with the driver even if the car is stopped. When you reach an intersection, wait behind the first car at the traffic light. Don't move up next to that car; drivers don't always use turn signals, so you don't know for sure which way the car will turn when the light turns green.

Negotiating sidewalks and bike paths. Many people consider sidewalks safe places to ride, because cars don't travel on them. Unfortunately, sidewalks aren't safe. Stay off them, except where you have no choice.

Trees, hedges, parked cars, buildings, and doorways create blind spots along a sidewalk, which is too narrow to allow you to swerve out of the way if someone appears. A pedestrian on the sidewalk can sidestep suddenly, or a small child can run out from behind an adult. Never pass a pedestrian until you have his attention.

A bike path can have all the same problems as a sidewalk. Even if bicycles are supposed to have the right of way, the path may be too narrow for safe maneuvering. Pedestrians are just as unpredictable, and intersections are often hazardous.

Avoiding the moving blindspot. On your bicycle, you can see over most cars. You'll become used to this advantage. Don't let it fool you, though. You can't see over a large van, truck, or bus.

Suppose that you're riding on a two-way, four-lane street. You've merged to the inside lane because you want to turn left. You signal your left turn and continue to move forward. You see only one other vehicle on the street: a van, coming toward you in the opposite passing lane. It stops to let you turn left. Can you make your turn safely?

No! Since you are moving forward, a blind spot behind the van is "moving toward you." A car could be passing the van in the outside lane, and you would never see that car. If you were to cross in front of the van, you could be met with a terrible surprise.

Making sure drivers know you exist. People will often tell you to "ride as if you were invisible." Instead, ride to make sure you're visible. Wear bright-colored clothes by day, and use lights and reflectors at night. Also, ensure that drivers have seen you, even if it means calling out to get a driver's attention.

MOUNTAIN BIKING SKILLS

Go to any mountain bike race and you'll soon be amazed at how some riders glide over terrain while others blithely blunder along, bouncing their front wheels off rocks and desperately trying to muscle their bikes. But good mountain bikers flow along a trail like water down a streambed. How do they perform this sleight-of-wheel?

By tapping into the "flow." Flow isn't so much a physical skill as a mindset. Keep these three things in mind, and you'll be flowing in no time.

Anticipation. Your body tends to move in the direction your eyes are focused. Stare doggedly a few feet ahead of your front wheel, and you'll have to make split-second decisions to avoid obstacles.

But if you make a habit of looking 20 or 30 feet up the trail, you'll ride smoothly, without the tension and fatigue that ruin flow. Pretend you have two sets of eyes. One pair sees the big picture, helping you pick the best line through obstacles. The other pair detects all the trail's subtle details so you can make tiny adjustments along the way. Concentrate mostly on your big-picture focus by looking well ahead of your bike. Then trust your peripheral vision to avoid rocks and roots. Keep your head up and most of your attention focused well down the trail, and your bike will flow along the line of your gaze.

Balance. Flow depends mightily on balance—a sense of where your weight is on the bike—particularly on steep climbs. Try to be like a cat. When a feline is poised to pounce, it's loose, not rigid. Practice catlike balance when rolling slowly along on a grassy surface. Like a feline, get on all fours—weight on hands and feet, buttocks off the saddle. Then pounce by jumping the bike from your balanced position. There's no need to get big air. Just get both wheels a couple inches off the ground, roll ahead a few feet, and repeat. Relax. As you improve, go slower.

Calm. A relaxed body creates a relaxed mind. If your handgrip is loose and your shoulders are flexible, your nature can become calm, ready for anything the trail throws at you. Avoid the panicked "oh-no" response as you look ahead. Instead, think, "I can help my bike get over this obstacle."

Here's how to practice: Find a section of trail with an obstacle, like a water bar or a rock ledge, that you're having trouble cleaning. It should be something you make maybe 4 or 5 times out of 10—the sort of challenge that makes you tense up when you spot it looming around the corner. Take a couple deep breaths and ride it as slowly as possible. Work on timing. It's easy to relax because, at such a slow speed, you can just put a foot down if you need to. As you get better, increase speed a little, but don't lose that feeling of calm. Soon, you'll be flowing over the ledge.

Which Line Would You Choose—A or B?

Squeeze between rock and tree

Do you feel lucky?

Don't widen trail; ride between rocks

Rocky, twisted, short climb

Flat trail, soft leaves, no surprises

Build momentum; ride over rock

Mud bog: Straight through, weight back

Wheel trap: Stay out

A B

Choose A and you'll have an easy time—until you stop dead at the wall of wood. Choose B and you face rocks, roots, narrow passages, and a short climb—but it's doable and fun.

BIKE ACCESSORIES
YOU NEED

Whether you're budgeting for a new bike or dusting off one you haven't ridden in a while, be sure to set aside some money for accessories. All of the following items will improve your cycling experience, but they've been prioritized to help you choose wisely. Included are things you "must have" for safe, enjoyable cycling and those you "should have" to increase comfort, speed, or convenience.

Must Have

Helmet ($30 to $130). Modern expanded-polystyrene helmets are light, cool, and attractive. Two innovations have become popular: a detachable visor to shield your face against sun, rain, mud, and branches, and a lightweight "locking" device that extends from the rear of the helmet to hug the back of your head, providing a firmer fit. Check for an ANSI, ASTM, or Snell sticker inside to be sure the helmet meets current safety standards. If you already have a helmet, but it's several years old, be aware that manufacturers say that foam degrades with time and becomes less able to absorb impacts. Consider buying a fresh helmet, which is also likely to be lighter, better ventilated, and more stylish than your old one.

Water bottle and cage ($7 to $25). The cardinal rules of hydration are to drink before you're thirsty and to down at least one bottle (22 ounces) every hour. Most frames have mounts for two cages, so if you sweat a lot or ride for more than 60 minutes, buy a pair.

Flat repair kit ($15). Don't press your luck. Every rider will get a flat, so you need to carry the necessary repair items. Your kit should include tire levers for removing the tire, a tube that matches your valve type and tire size, and a tube patch kit. Add two pieces of canvas for covering large slits in the tire casing from the inside.

Seatbag ($7 to $20). Choose one that's big enough to hold your flat repair kit and whatever else you like to carry. Some models have zippers that expand their capacity—great for stuffing that jacket when the day warms up.

Frame-fit pump ($20 to $50). Buy one that's the proper length to fit your frame and that has the correct valve type or is reversible. Also consider a minipump, which costs about the same but is less than half the length and mounts with clips that go under your bottle cage. A minipump doesn't inflate as quickly as a frame-fit pump, but it's lighter and more portable. You can carry it with you when you leave your bike in public.

Should Have

Lock ($15 to $85). U-locks offer the best security, but they're heavy and require removing the front wheel. Cables with padlocks are sufficient for occasional use in low-risk areas. If you plan to lock your bike frequently in public places, consider using both a U-lock and a cable lock. Always lock your bike to an immovable object, not just to itself.

Headlight ($30 to $300) and reflective material ($5 to $15). All states require lights after dark. For frequent night riding, consider a premium rechargeable headlight as well as a battery-powered flashing taillight ($10 to $20). Apply reflective tape to your frame, helmet, crankarms, and rims, and consider a reflective vest ($15). For night riding on well-lit streets, you may need only an inexpensive light that makes you noticeable to motorists.

Tool kit or all-in-one tool ($15 to $80). This should include screwdrivers, a small adjustable wrench, allen wrenches, a chain rivet extractor, and a spoke wrench. Keep it in your seatbag.

Gloves ($10 to $35). These have half-fingers and padded palms, which increase comfort and reduce abrasions in a crash. Choose a model with terry cloth on the thumb or back so that you can wipe your nose or eyes during rides. White or bright colors make you more noticeable to traffic when giving hand signals.

Shoes ($50 to $250). The soles are extra-stiff to prevent foot pain and numbness from pedal pressure, while transferring more of your power to turning the crankarms. Touring and mountain bike shoes have ridged or knobby soles that can be walked in fairly comfortably. Shoes with cleats that snap into the pedals offer the best power link, but they are more awkward for walking unless the cleats are recessed in the soles.

Toe clips and straps ($10 to $60) or clipless pedals ($80 to $250). These improve efficiency and prevent your feet from slipping off. Clipless pedals work like ski bindings, releasing your feet in the event of a fall. Some models allow your feet to pivot freely a few degrees, reducing the risk of knee strain.

EQUIPMENT-REPAIR

CLOTHING FOR
COLD-WEATHER RIDES

No matter how hot it gets in summer, cyclists always create a cooling breeze simply by rolling down the road. But take that same pace and combine it with temperatures in the thirties, and suddenly speed chills.

To enjoy cycling year round, you need clothing that blocks wind and retains warmth without making you overheat.

Head. More body heat is lost through the neck and head than through any other avenue. Protecting them is priority one, and it's easy (and cheap). A great choice is a polypropylene balaclava that's thin enough not to require changing helmet pads. You can leave its vents uncovered, allowing air flow to prevent a sweaty head, a danger on climbs. The balaclava fits tight around your face and can extend well into a turtleneck undershirt to provide a double layer on your neck and prevent air leaks. When necessary, you can pull it up to cover your chin or mouth. It's effective in a wide range of temperatures and can easily be stuffed into a pocket if the temperature climbs.

Feet. These are the first body parts to announce displeasure in cold temperatures. Interestingly, you'll have a better chance of keeping your toes toasty if your head and torso are warm. Wear socks made of an insulating material that holds moisture away from your skin. Wool hightops are good, but synthetics such as Polartec, Thermax, and various blends work well, too. Be careful not to fasten your shoes too tight, restricting circulation. Then cover them with booties. Some of the most effective and reasonably priced are made of neoprene. For maximum heat retention, choose booties that have high tops that fit snugly around your ankles, with cleat cutouts no larger than necessary.

Hands. Again, keep your core warm, and your hands will have a better chance. For temperatures above 35°F, full-finger gloves will do. But when it's colder, nothing works as well as insulated "lobster" gloves that put two fingers and your thumb in one compartment and your other two fingers in another. This enhances warmth almost as well as full mittens but allows the dexterity to operate a bike. Other features of good winter gloves include long, stretchy cuffs to prevent air leaks, terry material on the backs for wiping your nose, and windproof, water-resistant shells. The trick with the "lobster" type is knowing the temperature above which they'll be too warm. If your hands sweat, the dampness can make the gloves feel chilly.

Torso. Dress in layers that transport moisture and trap body heat. Start with a polypro undershirt, then put on a long-sleeve turtleneck made of polypro or another wicking, insulating material. On top, wear a wool/acrylic-blend jacket with nylon chest panels. This blocks the wind while allowing the back of the jacket to release body heat, reducing the risk of getting too warm. A full-length front zipper lets you open the jacket while climbing or riding with a tailwind.

On cold, rainy days, wear a waterproof jacket with underarm vents. You may get damp inside (from sweat and condensation), but you'll stay warm.

Wear a small fanny pack around the outside of your jacket. This will hold it down, keeping your lower back covered and allowing you to work the front zipper easily with one hand. Also, it gives you a way to carry small items, since you don't have jersey pockets.

Legs. Working legs don't need as much protection as a static torso does. Above about 45°F, leg warmers generally feel better than tights. They let your hips breathe to reduce the chance of becoming too warm. If it's chillier, switch to polypro or brushed Lycra tights. When the temperature is 30°F or colder, use tights with a bib top for extra torso and lower-back insulation. You can also get these with double-thick knee panels for additional protection.

Windchill Chart

Wind (mph)	Temperature (°F)												
0	35	30	25	20	15	10	5	0	–5	–10	–15	–20	–25	–30
	Equivalent Temperature												
5	33	27	21	16	12	7	1	–6	–11	–15	–20	–26	–31	–35
10	21	16	9	2	–2	–9	–15	–22	–27	–31	–38	–45	–52	–58
15	16	11	1	–6	–11	–18	–25	–33	–40	–45	–51	–60	–65	–70
20	12	3	–4	–9	–17	–24	–32	–40	–46	–52	–60	–68	–76	–81
25	7	0	–7	–15	–22	–29	–37	–45	–52	–58	–67	–75	–83	–89
30	5	–2	–11	–18	–26	–33	–41	–49	–56	–63	–70	–78	–87	–94
35	3	–4	–13	–20	–27	–35	–43	–52	–60	–67	–72	–83	–90	–98
40	1	–4	–15	–22	–29	–36	–45	–54	–62	–69	–76	–87	–94	–101

QUICK AND EASY
TUNE-UP: ROAD BIKE

This routine tune-up should take about an hour. Once you have the tools, it's manageable by the average home mechanic. Keep in mind that this procedure works only on reasonably maintained bikes in good condition. If yours is beat from years of abuse, it may need a complete overhaul (including repacking bearings).

To help you get started, here's a list of all the tools you'll need to complete a tune-up.

Repair stand	4-, 5-, and 6-mm allen wrenches
Spray cleaner/polish	Awl
Rags	Spoke wrench
Long screwdriver	Pump
Degreaser	Grease
Bucket	Lube
Detergent	Crankarm bolt wrench
Sponges	Pedal wrench
Headset wrenches	10-mm combination wrench
Large adjustable wrench	Brake or cone wrench

1. **Clean the bike.** Place it in a repair stand (outside, if possible). If it's only slightly dirty, apply a spray cleaner/polish made for bicycles to the frame and parts, then wipe with a clean rag. For a filthy bike, remove both wheels, and put a long screwdriver through the triangular hole in the rear dropouts and chain so the chain is held up. Spray the chain and derailleurs with degreaser and let the bike sit for a few minutes. Fill the bucket with warm soapy water. Douse an old sponge, hold it on the chain, and turn the crankarm to draw the chain through the sponge until the links sparkle. Clean the crankset and derailleurs, as well. Then clean the frame and parts (including wheels) with a fresh sponge. When everything is clean, rinse

by dribbling water from above. (Don't spray directly at the bike, because this can force water into the bearings.) Dry the bike and parts with rags.

2. **Check the bearings.** Stand in front of the bike, holding the fork in one hand and the down tube in the other. Push and pull on the fork to check for play in the headset bearings. Turn the fork slowly from side to side to feel for roughness. If it's loose or tight, adjust nut-style headsets by loosening the top nut with a headset wrench or large adjustable wrench, then slightly tighten or loosen the cone (underneath the top nut) with another. Next, tighten the top nut against the cone while you hold it in place (see photo). For a threadless headset, loosen the stem binder bolt, then remove play or tightness by adjusting the allen screw atop the stem, and finish by securing the stem bolts.

Now check the bottom bracket bearings. Stand beside the frame, hold the crankarms, and push and pull, feeling for play. Most modern bottom brackets are sealed and reliable. If yours is loose, have a shop remove the crankarms and adjust it. Finally, check the hub bearings. If the wheels are in the frame, grasp each rim and wiggle it laterally to feel for looseness. If the wheels are out, remove the quick-release skewers and turn and wiggle each axle with your fingers. Should there be looseness or binding, take the wheels to the shop for service.

3. **Inspect the tires.** Look for sidewall cracks, tread cuts, bald tread, or other damage. Search for objects embedded in the tread. Pick them out with an awl, or they could work their way through and cause a puncture. Inflate both tires to the pressure marked on the sidewall. Install the wheels on the bike, making sure they're centered in the frame.

4. **True the wheels.** Starting at the valve, work your way around each wheel, grabbing and wiggling spokes to see if any are loose. After

a few spokes, you'll get a feel for correct tension. Keep in mind that the left-side spokes on the rear wheel are always looser than the others—just make sure they're evenly tensioned compared to each other. If you find a loose spoke, tighten it with a spoke wrench by turning the nipple clockwise (when sighted from above) in half-turn increments until it's tensioned like its neighbors. Then spin the wheels and sight trueness by looking at the

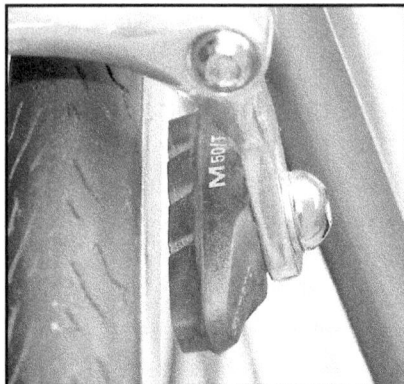

gap between the rim and brake pad (see photo). True the wheels, if necessary. To move the rim to the left, loosen right-side nipples and tighten left-side nipples in the problem area. Do the reverse to move the rim to the right. Always turn nipples half a turn at a time and check progress.

5. **Snug all parts.** Though major components shouldn't loosen with normal use, it's wise to check them with the appropriate tools. Without forcing, try to tighten both crankarm bolts, pedals, chainring bolts (don't forget those for the granny gear if you have triple chainrings), stem binder, handlebar binder, seat binder, seat bolt brake- and derailleur-attaching nuts or bolts, and the bottle cage or rack screws. (Everything is turned clockwise to tighten except the left pedal, which is turned counterclockwise.)

Finally, put a drop of lube on the pivot points of clipless pedals, derailleurs, and brakes.

6. **Adjust the shifting.** Lube shift cables where they pass the bottom bracket. Lube the chain, then shift through the gears repeatedly to test derailleur adjustments. Because the rear derailleur's cable is longer and gets more use, it's more likely to go out of adjustment. Each click of the rear shift lever should cause the chain to immediately jump to the next cog. If not, the cable has probably stretched slightly, or you may have mistakenly adjusted it too tightly. If the chain hesitates to go to a larger cog, the cable is slightly loose. If it hesitates to go to a smaller cog, it

is slightly tight. Fix slow shifts to larger cogs by turning the adjustment barrel on the rear of the derailleur counterclockwise in half-turn increments (see photo). For slow shifts to smaller cogs, turn the barrel clockwise.

7. **Inspect brake pads.** If the grooves are almost worn away, replace the pads. Make sure they strike the rim squarely. If they don't, loosen the nut with an allen or 10-mm wrench and reposition them. Squeeze the brake levers to feel the action. The pads should strike the rim well before the levers approach the handlebar. If not, tighten the brake by turning the barrel on the brake caliper. If it's one piece, turn it counterclockwise until the pads are ⅛ to ¼ inch away from the rim. If the barrel has two pieces, turn the ring on the barrel clockwise to tighten the brake (you might have to lift the barrel to get the ring to turn). If the pads don't release equally, center the brake with the small screw above the brake arm (on Shimano brakes) or allen on the side of the brake arm (on Campagnolo brakes).

8. **Test-ride the bike.** Shift and brake repeatedly, then fine-tune adjustments, if necessary. If the brakes squeal, determine which one is making the noise. Adjust its pads by toeing them slightly. Make the front end contact the rim first. Position the pad to produce a 1-mm gap between the back of the pad and the rim (on contact), then tighten

the nut. If the pads don't have toeing hardware, it's possible to adjust them by bending the brake arm with an adjustable wrench (see photo). Open the jaws just enough to slide them over the arm. Go easy so you don't break the brake.

QUICK AND EASY
TUNE-UP: MOUNTAIN BIKE

Though touted as indestructible, mountain bikes do need regular tune-ups. In fact, if they're ridden regularly or aggressively off road, they'll need even more service (about every six months) than road machines do. The mud, crud, and sludge found in the outback can foul things quickly. If you keep the bike clean, lubed, and adjusted according to these instructions, it will ride better and last longer.

This quick tune-up isn't appropriate for a thrashed bike. If your rig has gone a year without service, the wheels are bent, the cables and housings are frayed or cracked, or the chain is frozen with rust, you should take the bike to a good shop for an overhaul. Once everything is back in order, use this tune-up procedure to keep it that way.

Gather up the following tools, and you'll be ready to get your bike back in shape.

Bucket	Lube
Detergent	Pump
Repair stand	Spoke wrench
Newspapers	Acetone
Degreaser	Crankarm bolt wrench
Sponges	4-, 5-, 6-, and 8-mm allen wrenches
Brushes	Pedal wrench
Rags	Grease
Small regular screwdriver	

1. **Wash the bike.** Fill a bucket with warm soapy water. Put the bike in a repair stand outside, or spread newspapers beneath it. Shift to the largest chainring and middle cog. Coat the chain with degreaser and let it sit. Then scrub it by pedaling the bike while squeezing a sponge on the chain until it's clean. Now, shift to the

smallest ring/smallest cog combination, release the brake crossover cables, open the hub quick-releases, and remove the wheels. Refill the bucket. Scrub the bike and wheels with a clean sponge and brushes.

2. **Apply degreaser to the chainrings and cogs.** Move a rag's edge in a shoeshine motion to clean between them. If dirt or grass is stuffed between the cogs, dig it out with a small screwdriver. When you wash the wheels, pay special attention to the tire sidewalls. Look for cuts or fraying threads that indicate the tire should be replaced. To rinse the bike, drip water on the frame and wheels from above. Then dry the frame, components, and wheels with rags. Finally, lube the chain.

3. **Check the headset and lube the cables.** Most modern mountain bikes have threadless headsets, which are easier to service than conventional types. Check yours by standing in front of the bike, grabbing the fork, and pushing and pulling gently. If there's any play, loosen the stem binder bolt with an allen wrench, turn the screw atop the stem clockwise just enough to eliminate play, and tighten the stem bolts. If this doesn't work, have the adjustment checked by a shop mechanic.

If there are bare cable sections, relube the cables by releasing the housing ends from the stops. If the ends are stuck, push them out with a screwdriver (see photo). For the rear brake, pull on the housing and lift it out of the stops. Free the other housing section similarly. Then slide the housing aside and lube the newly exposed portion of cable. For derailleur cables, push the derailleur inward to create slack. Then lift the housing out of the frame stops, slide it down the cable, and lube the exposed section. If you can't release the housings, your cables are probably sealed and don't need lube.

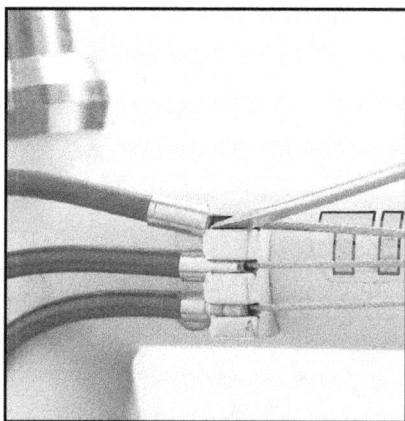

4. Inflate the tires and reinstall the wheels. Make sure they're fully inserted, centered in the frame, and that their quick-releases are tight. Check for loose spokes. Start at the valve and wiggle each one. Keep in mind that the left-side spokes on the rear wheel are looser than the other three sets. Compare them only to each other. If you find loose spokes, tighten them by turning the nipples in half-turn increments until they're as tight as adjacent ones.

Then spin the wheels to gauge trueness. Hold your thumb against a brake or the frame and watch the gap between your thumb and the rim. To move the rim to the right, loosen the left nipples and tighten the right ones in half-turn increments (when viewed from outside the rim) until the wobble is gone (see photo). Repeat until the wheels are true. Clean the rims with acetone to remove brake-pad deposits.

5. Tighten everything. Major components can loosen from the rigors of trail riding, so check everything with the appropriate tools. Don't force—but try to tighten—the following: both crankarm bolts, pedals (remember that the left one tightens counterclockwise), chainring bolts (don't forget those for the small ring), the stem binder, handlebar binder, bar-end binders, seat binder, seat bolt, brake and derailleur nuts or bolts, brake- and shift-lever bolts, and water bottle and rack screws.

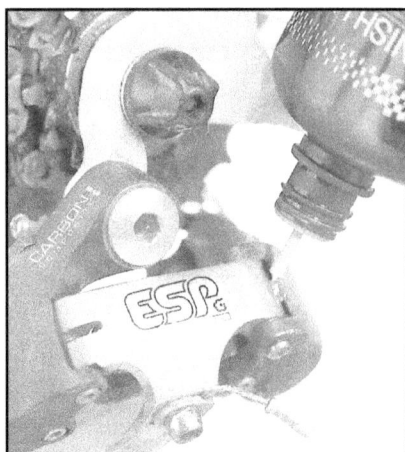

Also, remove, clean, and test your frame pump. If it's not pumping, try unscrewing the top, extracting the rod, and adding grease to the plunger. Check your patch kit: Still have patches? Has the glue evaporated? Lube the pivot points of clipless pedals, front and rear derailleurs (see photo), and brakes.

6. **Check derailleur adjustments.** Shift through all the gear combinations. Hesitation when shifting to larger cogs is a sign that the cable has stretched. To speed shifts, turn the adjusting barrel on the back of the derailleur counter-clockwise half a turn and recheck. Repeat until the derailleur shifts to the next cog with each click of the lever. If shifts to larger chainrings aren't crisp, perform the same fix for the front derailleur by turning the adjusting barrel on the shift lever (see photo).

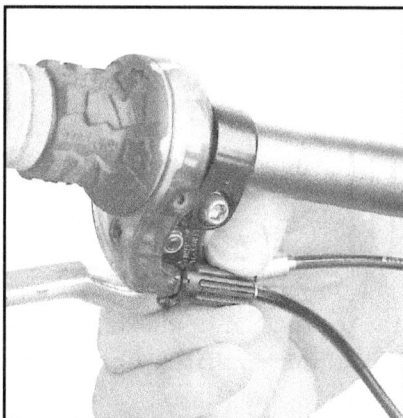

7. **Check brake pads.** These are the parts that wear quickest on mountain bikes, especially if you're a mud monster. Check the surface of each pad. There should be grooves. If not, the pads are worn and should be replaced. To replace them, look for adjusting barrels on the brake levers and thread them in fully. (You might have to loosen a locknut first.) Then replace the pads individually. Copy the position of the opposite pad as closely as possible, and tighten the locknut to secure it.

To check the position, push the brake arm in and note how the pad strikes the rim. It should hit squarely but be angled just a tad so the front tip touches first. If it doesn't, loosen the nut and reposition the pad. Hook up the crossover cable and squeeze the brake levers to check feel. If you like less lever play, unscrew the adjustment barrels slightly and hold their position with the locknut (if available).

8. **Service the suspension.** If you have suspension on your bike—front, rear, or both—check the owner's manual to see what service is required. For instance, the pressure should be checked regularly on air shocks, and elastomer forks should be disassembled, cleaned, and lubed. The pivots on dual-suspension frames can loosen and should be secured or lubed. If you don't have the owner's manual, contact a local shop for advice or call the company that built your bike or shock.

How to Prevent Equipment Failures

Why do parts break? The manufacturer's favorite explanation is abuse. It's true: When you crash your mountain bike into a tree, you're abusing the bike and the damage is your fault, not the bike's.

On the other hand, the blame for some failures may indeed rest with the part maker. In the ideal scenario, new parts go through a lengthy, detailed process that involves designing, testing, prototype-building, more testing, manufacturing of production parts, and more testing. Often, however, this ideal process is rushed.

Here are some guidelines for what can go wrong out there and how you can prevent problems.

Cranksets/Bottom Brackets

What to look out for: For cranksets, check for small cracks by the pedal hole, at the spider end of the right crankarm, or around the crankarm hole (taper). Potential bottom-bracket problems can be hard to spot; pay attention to noises during hard pedaling.

How long they last: Theoretically, cranksets last forever. But we see broken ones all the time. Steel bottom-bracket sets are extremely durable; lightweight titanium replacements should be checked regularly.

Recommendations: We feel safest on cold-forged aluminum cranksets from famous makers. Steel bottom-bracket axles are best, but well-made 6AI/4V titanium axles can be strong.

Handlebars

What to look out for: Beware of cracks near the stem clamp or next to the ferrule (center portion) of drop handlebars.

How long they last: Bars hit the ground a lot, so not too long; say, two seasons.

Recommendations: Mountain bike bars have been one of the most controversial—and dangerous—products in the "light" category. If you elect to

42

purchase a mountain bike bar weighing less than 150 grams, use caution. Also, use care when installing bar-ends, brake levers, and shifters, which can cause small scratches that spread and lead to failure. (Some bar makers prohibit the use of bar-ends with their products or supply special inserts to reinforce that portion of the bar.) Never buy a used mountain bike bar. In general, buy a famous brand of mountain bike or road bar, and don't crash or drop your bike.

Pedals

What to look out for: Inspect the spindle area near the crankarm for cracks.

How long they last: Pedals have a life span of five years with regular maintenance and not too many crashes.

Recommendations: We prefer brands from famous makers with chrome-moly steel (rather than titanium) axles. If you use an after-market titanium replacement axle, check it regularly for cracks or excessive wear.

Road Forks

What to look out for: Cracks by the dropouts, at the base of the steerer, along the fork legs, or where the legs join the crown are signs of trouble.

How long they last: Quality models that haven't been crashed can last indefinitely.

Recommendations: Steel models last longest (but also can break). Composite and aluminum ones should be checked regularly and replaced if they have cracks, corrosion, audible creaking, or other signs of wear. Some new forks are dipping under the one-pound barrier; pay special attention to these superlight models. Any fork that has experienced a frontal impact should be considered suspect, or better yet, tossed. Eye road bikes from the side, to ensure that the upper part of the blades are in line with the head tube. Unusual shoe overlap when turning the wheel can be another sign that the bike underwent frontal impact.

How to Fix Something with Nothing

Great day for a ride. You have your mini-tool, plenty of water, food, and a jacket. But you weren't expecting to endo and fracture your frame and handlebar or find that your patch-kit glue dried up. Fear not. We're here to help, with tips on fixing things when all seems lost.

You shift into low and the bike won't go. Instead, there's a sickening crunch as the rear wheel eats your derailleur, bending the frame's hanger. Dave McLaughlin, manager of the Schwinn-Toyota pro team, says, "Remove the rear wheel and derailleur. Unscrew the cap end of the quick-release skewer, and thread the end of the axle into the hanger. Screw on the quick-release cap until tight. Then use the wheel as a lever to straighten the derailleur hanger" (see photo). This works best on steel frames. Go gently on aluminum and titanium. Have the alignment checked by a shop soon.

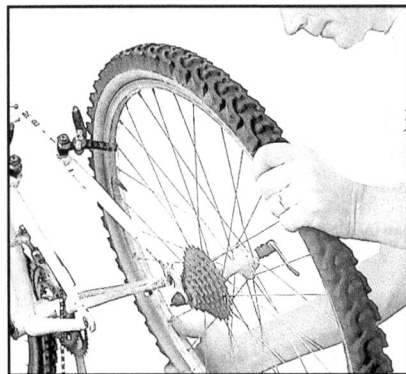

You toast the rear derailleur by shifting into the spokes or hitting boulders. Detach the cable, separate the chain, remove the rear derailleur, and place the chain in an easy gear (middle chainring/middle cog). Remove links, as necessary, to achieve a taut chain in whichever gear you select, and rejoin the chain. Now you have a one-speed that you can pedal home. Check the chain for bends. If possible, remove or straighten the bad section.

Some accessory—a fender, rack, light, or pump—loses a bolt and starts rattling or falling off. Zip-ties work great to stop the rattling or reattach the accessories. Zip-ties are cheap. Buy a few and tuck them in your pack.

The chainring or crankarm bolt falls off. Whittle a replacement out of wood with a knife. Then press or thread the part in place. Pedal lightly on loosely affixed crankarms, as hard use will ruin them.

You incur serious tire or tube damage. To fix a bad tube, cut it at the puncture, tie the two ends together in a knot, and reinstall it. For tire cuts that allow the tube to bulge and blow out, carry a small supply of duct tape, which is adhesive, so it's easy to apply. Or use energy bar wrappers to boot tire cuts. Don't have any? Use cash. Dollar bills are made of linen, not paper. Weakened tubes and tires can blow. Take it easy, and get new rubber for your bike as soon as possible.

Twang! A shift cable breaks. As long as the cable is still attached to the derailleur, pull the cable until the bike is in a good pedaling gear, and then hold it in place by clamping the cable beneath any convenient screw, such as one securing the water bottle cage (see photo). You can even shift a bit by pulling on the cable.

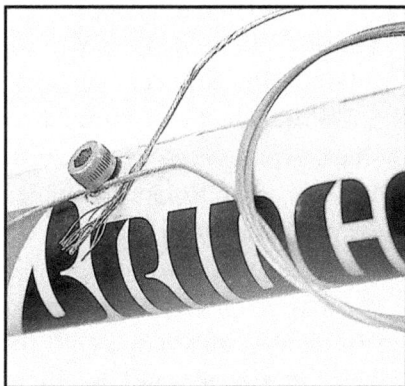

You survive a death-defying descent, but one of your main frame tubes breaks. Franjo Goluza, editor of the Internet-based *Road 'N' Grime* magazine out of British Columbia, says he "splints the broken tube by placing a stick next to it and wrapping the piece of wood and the frame tube together with a spare tube, then securing the ends with shoelaces. But you can also use an aluminum can and wire found by the road. Cut the can into a long one-inch strip, wrap it around the frame, and secure it by wrapping it with the wire." Broken bikes ride sketchy, so keep the speed down.

Left the tire levers at home. Quick-releases make dandy tire levers. And most mountain bike tires can be removed by hand.

FIX A FLAT FAST

ooner or later, it'll happen. You'll be pedaling along when you'll hear hissing or a sudden kapow, and one end of the bike will sink. Yep, it's a flat tire, the most common breakdown you'll face as a cyclist.

We're assuming that you'll have a flat while riding. If you're working at home and have access to a repair stand, by all means use it. On the road, it's not necessary to support the bike, but you may be able to by hooking the nose of the saddle over a fence or low branch. Or ask a riding partner to hold the bike while you operate.

Always carry the following tools in your seatbag so you're prepared to make repairs: tire levers, a spare tube sized for your tires, a rag, and a pocketknife. Plus, keep your bike equipped with a frame-fit pump.

1. **Open the brake.** To make it easy to remove the wheel and put it back in, most brakes can be widened. For a cantilever, squeeze both brake pads against the rim with one hand, and unhook the transverse cable from the brake arm (see photo, left). For sidepulls, look for a lever on the caliper (see photo, right) or lever handle, and open it to spread the pads.

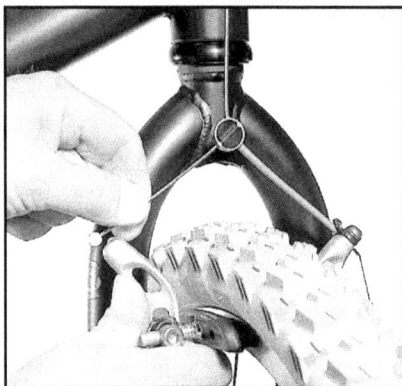

2. Remove the wheel. Most bikes have quick-release (QR) hubs so wheels can be removed without tools. If it's a rear flat, shift onto the smallest cog to move the derailleur to the side. To remove either wheel, open its QR by flipping the lever 180 degrees. You should feel it loosen, and you may see the word "open" on the lever. It helps to pull the derailleur back with one hand as you push the wheel forward and down with the other (see photo). Front wheels won't necessarily come off when the QR is opened. Many bikes have nubs on the fork dropouts that capture the QR to prevent the wheel from dislodging if the lever is improperly tightened. If this is your setup, hold either end of the QR and unscrew the other until it clears the nubs. Then remove the wheel.

3. Remove the tire. If any air remains, deflate the tube completely. Depress a Schrader valve with the corner of a tire lever; unscrew and depress the top of a presta valve. Then hold the wheel upright, and slide a tire lever under one side of the bead, 180 degrees from the valve stem. Pull the lever down to pry the bead off the rim, and hold it or hook it to a spoke. Place the second lever under the same bead, about four inches from the first lever, and pull it down (see photo). Repeat the process, leapfrogging the levers. Soon, you should be able to slide a lever around the rim to free that entire side of the tire. Then reach inside and extract the tube, except where the valve stem goes through the rim. Go 180 degrees from the valve and pull the tire up and off the rim. (Use the levers if it's tight.) Note: A presta valve may be held through the rim by a nut or knurled ring, which must be unscrewed before the tube can be completely removed.

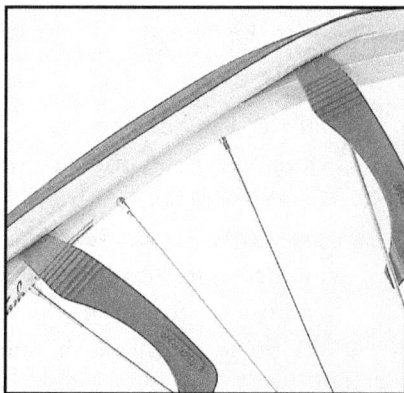

4. Replace the tube. The easiest way to fix a flat is to replace the tube. Save the punctured one to patch at home, then make it your spare. Before installing a fresh tube, you must check the tire to see if whatever caused the flat is still sticking through. A good way is to

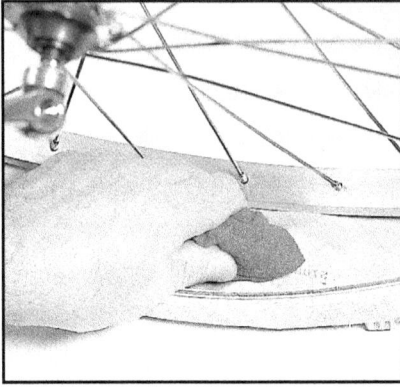

wad a rag and slowly slide it inside the tire in both directions (see photo). It will catch on anything sharp, which you can pick out with a pocketknife. Next, inflate the fresh tube just enough to remove wrinkles, and feed it into the tire. For a pro look, align the valve stem with the tire label.

5. Install the tire. Lay the wheel on its side and place the tire/tube combo on top, with the valve stem at the valve hole. Start installation by putting the stem partially through and working the lower bead onto the rim all the way around. If the stem won't go, the rim strip's hole is probably off center. To mount the second bead, start at the stem and work the tire over the rim with both hands. The last section can be tough. It helps to fully deflate the tube, place the wheel on your knee, hold one end of the uninstalled section to keep it in place, then use the heel of your stronger hand to roll the bead up and over. Use tire levers as a last resort, because there's danger of pinching a hole in the tube. After the tire is mounted, go back to the valve stem and push it up into the tire to make sure the tube isn't caught under the beads, then pull it down.

6. Inflate. Place the pump on the valve. Brace it by wrapping your thumb over the tire and your finger behind a spoke so you won't bend or break the valve when pumping forcefully (see photo). Inflate to full pressure, then check for proper seating. A fine line molded into the tire sidewall (called the "bead line") should be equidistant from the rim all the way around on both sides. Spin the tire to eye this. If the line dives beneath or bows above the rim, deflate the tire and wiggle the bad section. Add air and recheck. An incorrectly seated bead will prevent the tire from rolling smoothly, and it could let the tube squeeze through and blow out. Sometimes you may have to carefully poke the tube from under the bead with a tire lever.

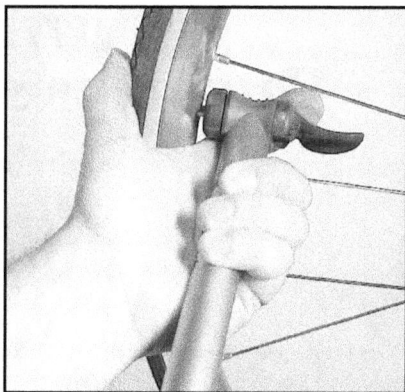

7. **Install the wheel.** For a front wheel, stand the bike up and place the wheel in the fork with the QR lever on the left. Make sure the wheel's axle is fully inserted in the dropouts. If you had to unscrew the QR to bypass dropout nubs, hold the lever open and turn the nut clockwise. The adjustment is correct when the QR begins to clamp after you've closed the lever about halfway. When fully closed, it should point up or to the rear, next to the fork blade. The force required should leave an impression on your palm. The procedure is similar for the rear wheel, but clamping the QR should be as easy as turning the lever (because you didn't need to change its adjustment to remove it). When installing a rear, remember to put the chain on the smallest cog, and make sure the wheel is centered between the chainstays and seatstays. Finish the job by hooking up the cantilever brake or closing the sidepull quick-release.

NUTRITION
QUESTIONS ANSWERED

Here are answers to the most frequent questions that cyclists ask about nutrition.

I lift weights and ride. Do I need extra protein—more than the recommended dietary allowance (RDA)?

Yes, both strength and endurance athletes need more protein than their couch-potato counterparts. Strength athletes need protein to build and repair muscle tissue, while the endurance folks need it to compensate for small amounts of protein used as fuel during exercise. The recommendation for athletes is 1.2 to 1.4 grams per kilogram (2.2 pounds) of body weight, compared to the RDA of 0.8 gram per kilogram. But unless you're a vegan (a vegetarian who eats no meat, dairy foods, or eggs) or you go overboard on carbohydrates, most diets provide close to 15 percent of calories as protein (more than 100 grams in 3,000 calories), which covers athletes' increased needs. Good protein sources include lean meat, low-fat dairy foods, eggs, and beans.

Do I need to take dietary supplements?

Generally, athletes who eat well (consuming the recommended amounts of protein and dairy products along with lots of fruits, vegetables, and whole grains) get sufficient vitamins and minerals. This is partly because athletes eat more than most people. So far, research hasn't shown clear performance-enhancing effects of extra vitamins or minerals.

Of course, there are exceptions. Women with heavy menstrual losses may need iron supplements, especially if they avoid red meat. If you're in this category, ask your doctor to keep tabs on your iron status. People who don't use dairy products usually need supplemental calcium for bone strength, and those who fall short on green leafy veggies might benefit from a folic acid supplement. Women who may become pregnant need folic acid to help prevent spina bifida in their infants. It may also decrease heart disease risks in both men and women.

Another exception could be vitamin E. There's less of it in a low-fat diet, and some research suggests that supplements of about 100 international units daily may help prevent heart disease. It's virtually impossible to get that much from food.

The bottom line? Consider a daily multivitamin/mineral and possibly a vitamin E supplement. But remember: No number of supplements can compensate for a poor diet.

Can the supplement creatine make me a stronger rider?

If you want to perform well at 30-second bouts of all-out riding, followed by four-minute rest periods—perhaps. Otherwise, probably not. In muscle, creatine combines with phosphate to form a temporary store of adenosine triphosphate (ATP), which is the immediate energy source for muscle contraction. ATP stores last for only a few seconds of all-out exercise, and creatine extends this for a few seconds more. Creatine supplements (20 grams a day for about five days) increase muscle creatine in cyclists having low-to-average levels to begin with.

Unfortunately, there's no easy way to know whether your muscle creatine is high or low. Levels vary widely. Those who limit or avoid meat often have low levels because creatine is found in flesh foods.

How does this relate to performance? Research results vary, but creatine does help athletes who have low to average muscle-creatine levels, and it improves short, all-out sprints. Most studies say there are no benefits in longer exercise bouts, even at intensities of up to 90 percent of max. Are you a sprinter with an eye for experimentation? Go for it. Creatine is legal and available in health food stores.

How do you eat while riding?

The best place to carry food is in the rear pockets of your jersey. To reach it, first grip the handlebar with one hand next to the stem to hold the bike steady. Then reach around with the other hand to grab the banana, which you can peel with your hand or teeth and eat. Another approach is to snack during rest stops. It's common for cyclists to stash food in seatbags or rack trunks for devouring at spontaneous roadside picnics.

NUTRITION

REACH YOUR IDEAL CYCLING WEIGHT

What's the best way to lose weight—and keep it off? First, take an objective look at your weight and body composition. Health experts recommend that your Body Mass Index (BMI) be between 19 and 25. BMI is a measure of relative weight calculated by dividing your body weight (in pounds) by the square of your height (in inches), then multiplying the total by 705. (For a shortcut, see the chart.)

Health risks from being overweight are believed to increase with a BMI above 27, but there's an important caveat: Research shows that overweight people who are fit actually have lower death rates than normal or underweight people who are unfit.

BMI measurements have a drawback: They don't reveal body composition. At a given BMI, body fat can vary considerably. For example, someone with a BMI of 26 and a relatively high fat level could improve cycling performance by shedding blubber. But a lean, muscular rider with the same BMI probably won't get the same benefit from losing weight. With little fat to lose, any weight loss would more likely come from muscle.

The Truth about Weight Loss

Keep on moving. Studies show that people who lose weight by burning excess calories with exercise are much more likely to maintain weight loss. Both aerobic exercise and strength training play a role. Increasing either the intensity or the duration of your cycling workouts increases energy expenditure. Adding resistance training two or three times a week increases not only calorie-burning but also strength that will help you get up that hill faster.

Watch what you eat. Limiting (but not eliminating) fat is important because we don't regulate fat calories as closely as we do calories from carbohydrate or protein. When carbo or protein intakes are increased, the body increases their oxidation (use for energy). But increases in fat don't lead to parallel increases in oxidation. The fat just gets stored on your body. The lesson? Carbos are key.

NUTRITION

Determining Body Mass Index

Height	Weight at BMI of 19 (lb.)	Weight at BMI of 25 (lb.)	Weight at BMI of 27 (lb.)
5'0"	97	128	138
5'1"	100	132	143
5'2"	104	136	147
5'3"	107	141	152
5'4"	110	145	157
5'5"	114	150	162
5'6"	117	155	167
5'7"	121	159	172
5'8"	125	164	177
5'9"	128	169	182
5'10"	132	174	188
5'11"	136	179	193
6'0"	140	184	199
6'1"	144	189	204
6'2"	148	194	210

Try increasing your fruit and vegetable intake to 10 servings (a serving is a half-cup chopped vegetables or a medium-size piece of fruit).

Eat early and eat often. If you're not a breakfast-eater, try being one for two weeks. Eating a good breakfast may prevent overeating later in the day. But don't skimp on dinner, either.

Write it down. If you're keeping tabs on your weight, the more frequently you write down what you eat, the more likely you are to lose weight or maintain your weight loss. Each time you chow down, a log helps you think twice about whether you're truly hungry or whether you're eating for some other reason.

Be patient. Weight loss should occur at a rate of between one-half and two pounds per week so that the lost weight isn't valuable muscle tissue. If you've lost 10 pounds, maintain the new weight for six months before attempting further weight loss. This may help your body recognize the new weight as its usual weight and prevent subsequent gain.

WHAT TO EAT BEFORE AND DURING LONG RIDES

Have a century or epic trail ride coming up? You may need to rethink your diet. If you're eating more protein and fat than carbohydrate or saving your carbo loading for the night before the ego-challenge, don't blame your body if it fails you en route.

For optimal energy, sports nutritionists recommend eating 55 to 65 percent of calories from carbohydrate, 10 to 15 percent from protein, and up to 30 percent as fat. An active cyclist should eat 3 to 4.5 grams of carbohydrate per day for each pound of body weight—about 450 to 675 grams of carbo for a 150-pound male. (Check food labels for carbo content.) That's a lot of carbohydrate, so try to get at least the minimum amount. Eat more if you're gearing up for a multiday endurance ride.

Pay attention to diet details the week before an important event. Contrary to popular belief, successful carbo loading isn't a preride pasta party. Instead, store more glycogen in your muscles during the three or four days before the big event by tapering exercise and eating primarily carbohydrates.

Go with what you know. Because everyone tolerates food before events differently, eat something familiar two to four hours before the start. Practice eating before training rides to get used to having something in your stomach. Don't skip breakfast. Pre-exercise high-carbo meals—liquids, solids, or sweets—have consistently proven to enhance performance.

Load up while you ride. Consume 30 to 60 grams of carbohydrate per hour while riding. That's about 16 ounces of most sports drinks. Eat energy bars, carbo gels, or your favorite pocket fuels for additional energy.

Make the most of your opportunity. According to research by Bill Strickland, contributing writer for *Bicycling* magazine, for a few hours after a ride of 90 minutes or longer, your body can convert carbohydrate into muscle glycogen faster than normal. Two hours after a ride, the rate of conversion is roughly cut in half. During the next two to four hours, it returns to

NUTRITION

normal. After this so-called glycogen window closes, you need an entire day—or more—to completely restock.

This means that if you miss the window and ride again within 24 hours, you're probably doing so with only partially energized muscles. You're weaker, and you'll tire sooner. But if you use the window, you can be sure you're cycling with the optimum amount of energy in your body. Taking advantage of this window is simple. It opens anytime you participate in an aerobic sport for longer than 90 minutes.

The Essential Element

During cycling, your muscles produce 30 to 100 times more heat than when you're at rest. Your body extinguishes this inferno primarily by increasing sweat rates. In summer, you can lose more than two liters (about 67 ounces) of fluid per hour on a hot day. If you don't replace it, power output declines in about 30 minutes.

Keep drinking. Cycling wisdom calls for one milliliter of fluid for every calorie you burn, according to Mitch Kanter, Ph.D., director of the Gatorade Sports Science Institute in Barrington, Illinois. "At about 3,500 calories a day, you'll need about 3½ liters. That's almost 15 eight-ounce glasses of fluid."

Prehydrate. Drink plenty of fluids every day, but before a race, long ride, or tour, start hyperhydrating at least 24 hours in advance.

Fill up again. After you've ridden for several hours, pump down fluids. What you drink makes a difference. Edward Coyle, Ph.D., director of the Human Performance Laboratory at the University of Texas in Austin, compared how dehydrated athletes who drank nearly two liters of either water, sports drink, or diet cola were affected two hours after exercise. Diet cola replenished 54 percent of fluid losses; water, 64 percent; and sports drinks, 69 percent.

Eat "wet" foods. About 60 percent of your daily fluid comes from the food you eat, but some foods increase hydration better than others. For instance, fruits and vegetables are great fluid sources—they're 80 to 95 percent water by weight.

Quench your thirst with sports drinks. Most popular sports drinks contain sodium, potassium, and other electrolytes. These are recommended for exercise lasting more than one hour. Whenever you plan to cycle for several hours, make sure you have two bottles of your favorite. Sports drinks are also useful for shorter workouts that include high-intensity riding.

Nutrition Log

eeping a food diary seems like a good idea, but it also seems like too much trouble. If you need incentive, try this: Cyclists who keep track of what they eat are more likely to lose weight than those who don't are. So we're going to make it easier for you.

For one week, make a point of writing down what you eat. On the opposite page, you'll find a nutrition log that asks you what you had for breakfast, lunch, dinner, and snacks each day. The key is to be completely honest. Don't change your regular eating habits just because you're keeping track for the week. That won't do you any good.

If you don't want to do all the math, compare your eating pattern with the Food Guide Pyramid that you will find on almost any item in your pantry. Think of it as a dietary cheat sheet, a visual guide reminding you of three concepts in one glance.

Variety: Eat lots of different stuff, hitting all the food groups.

Moderation: Watch your serving sizes, and go easy on the fats, oils, and sweets.

Proportion: Notice how big a block the grain and pasta group gets on the pyramid? Load up on those foods. See how much smaller the dairy group is? A little dab'll do ya.

You should be able to quickly tell whether your personal pyramid is top-heavy with fats and sugars or light on vegetables and grains. Make changes accordingly, then see whether you're doing any better six months later.

NUTRITION

56

Mon. breakfast   snacks

       lunch

       dinner

Tues. breakfast   snacks

       lunch

       dinner

Wed. breakfast   snacks

       lunch

       dinner

Thurs. breakfast   snacks

       lunch

       dinner

Fri. breakfast   snacks

       lunch

       dinner

Sat. breakfast   snacks

       lunch

       dinner

Sun. breakfast   snacks

       lunch

       dinner

NUTRITION

Monday

date   time   mileage

average speed   course   grade your ride

road   hilly   dry

a   b   c   d   e

mountain   flat   wet

cross-training   food/water

notes: _____

_____

_____

Tuesday

date   time   mileage

average speed   course   grade your ride

road   hilly   dry

a   b   c   d   e

mountain   flat   wet

cross-training   food/water

notes: _____

_____

_____

Wednesday

date   time   mileage

average speed   course   grade your ride

road   hilly   dry

a   b   c   d   e

mountain   flat   wet

cross-training   food/water

notes: _____

_____

_____

Thursday

date   time   mileage

average speed   course   grade your ride

road   hilly   dry

a   b   c   d   e

mountain   flat   wet

cross-training   food/water

notes: _____

_____

_____

TRAINING LOG

Friday
date   time   mileage

average speed   **course**   **grade your ride**

road hilly dry **a b c d e**

mountain flat wet

cross-training   food/water

notes: _____

_____

_____

Saturday
date   time   mileage

average speed   **course**   **grade your ride**

road hilly dry **a b c d e**

mountain flat wet

cross-training   food/water

notes: _____

_____

_____

Sunday
date   time   mileage

average speed   **course**   **grade your ride**

road hilly dry **a b c d e**

mountain flat wet

cross-training   food/water

notes: _____

_____

_____

Summary
weekly mileage   year to date

notes: _____

_____

_____

_____

Joining a bike club is the best and quickest way for a new rider to learn firsthand about the sport.

Monday

date   time   mileage

average speed   course   grade your ride

road   hilly   dry

a   b   c   d   e

mountain   flat   wet

cross-training   food/water

notes: _____

_____

_____

Tuesday

date   time   mileage

average speed   course   grade your ride

road   hilly   dry

a   b   c   d   e

mountain   flat   wet

cross-training   food/water

notes: _____

_____

_____

Wednesday

date   time   mileage

average speed   course   grade your ride

road   hilly   dry

a   b   c   d   e

mountain   flat   wet

cross-training   food/water

notes: _____

_____

_____

Thursday

date   time   mileage

average speed   course   grade your ride

road   hilly   dry

a   b   c   d   e

mountain   flat   wet

cross-training   food/water

notes: _____

_____

_____

TRAINING LOG

Friday

date   time   mileage

average speed   course   grade your ride

        road   hilly   dry

                         a b c d e

        mountain flat   wet

cross-training   food/water

notes: _____
_____
_____

Saturday

date   time   mileage

average speed   course   grade your ride

        road   hilly   dry

                         a b c d e

        mountain flat   wet

cross-training   food/water

notes: _____
_____
_____

Sunday

date   time   mileage

average speed   course   grade your ride

        road   hilly   dry

                         a b c d e

        mountain flat   wet

cross-training   food/water

notes: _____
_____
_____

Summary

weekly mileage   year to date

notes: _____
_____
_____
_____

Check all nuts and bolts on a new bike after the first week of use.
If anything is going to loosen, it'll usually happen during the initial miles.

TRAINING LOG

Monday

date   time   mileage

average speed   course   grade your ride

road   hilly   dry

a   b   c   d   e

mountain   flat   wet

cross-training   food/water

notes: _____
_____
_____

Tuesday

date   time   mileage

average speed   course   grade your ride

road   hilly   dry

a   b   c   d   e

mountain   flat   wet

cross-training   food/water

notes: _____
_____
_____

Wednesday

date   time   mileage

average speed   course   grade your ride

road   hilly   dry

a   b   c   d   e

mountain   flat   wet

cross-training   food/water

notes: _____
_____
_____

Thursday

date   time   mileage

average speed   course   grade your ride

road   hilly   dry

a   b   c   d   e

mountain   flat   wet

cross-training   food/water

notes: _____
_____
_____

Friday

date   time   mileage

average speed   course   grade your ride

road   hilly   dry

         a   b   c   d   e

mountain   flat   wet

cross-training   food/water

notes: _____
_____
_____

Saturday

date   time   mileage

average speed   course   grade your ride

road   hilly   dry

         a   b   c   d   e

mountain   flat   wet

cross-training   food/water

notes: _____
_____
_____

Sunday

date   time   mileage

average speed   course   grade your ride

road   hilly   dry

         a   b   c   d   e

mountain   flat   wet

cross-training   food/water

notes: _____
_____
_____

Summary

weekly mileage   year to date

notes: _____
_____
_____
_____

After a ride, brush your teeth before drinking and eating. This will cleanse your mouth of mucus, plus the dust, grit, and other airborne stuff that you've been breathing.

Monday

date   time   mileage

average speed   course   grade your ride

road   hilly   dry

a   b   c   d   e

mountain   flat   wet

cross-training   food/water

notes: _____

_____

_____

Tuesday

date   time   mileage

average speed   course   grade your ride

road   hilly   dry

a   b   c   d   e

mountain   flat   wet

cross-training   food/water

notes: _____

_____

_____

Wednesday

date   time   mileage

average speed   course   grade your ride

road   hilly   dry

a   b   c   d   e

mountain   flat   wet

cross-training   food/water

notes: _____

_____

_____

Thursday

date   time   mileage

average speed   course   grade your ride

road   hilly   dry

a   b   c   d   e

mountain   flat   wet

cross-training   food/water

notes: _____

_____

_____

Friday

date   time   mileage

average speed   course   grade your ride

road   hilly   dry

mountain   flat   wet

a   b   c   d   e

cross-training   food/water

notes: _____
_____
_____

Saturday

date   time   mileage

average speed   course   grade your ride

road   hilly   dry

mountain   flat   wet

a   b   c   d   e

cross-training   food/water

notes: _____
_____
_____

Sunday

date   time   mileage

average speed   course   grade your ride

road   hilly   dry

mountain   flat   wet

a   b   c   d   e

cross-training   food/water

notes: _____
_____
_____

Summary

weekly mileage   year to date

notes: _____
_____
_____
_____

Early in the season, take along a pruning saw every time you go trail riding. Stopping to clear a section takes just moments, and it'll make a better trail that you can enjoy throughout the summer.

Monday

date   time   mileage

average speed   course   grade your ride

road   hilly   dry

a b c d e

mountain   flat   wet

cross-training   food/water

notes: _____

_____

_____

Tuesday

date   time   mileage

average speed   course   grade your ride

road   hilly   dry

a b c d e

mountain   flat   wet

cross-training   food/water

notes: _____

_____

_____

Wednesday

date   time   mileage

average speed   course   grade your ride

road   hilly   dry

a b c d e

mountain   flat   wet

cross-training   food/water

notes: _____

_____

_____

Thursday

date   time   mileage

average speed   course   grade your ride

road   hilly   dry

a b c d e

mountain   flat   wet

cross-training   food/water

notes: _____

_____

_____

Friday

date   time   mileage

average speed   course   grade your ride

road   hilly   dry

       a   b   c   d   e

mountain   flat   wet

cross-training   food/water

notes: _____
_____
_____

Saturday

date   time   mileage

average speed   course   grade your ride

road   hilly   dry

       a   b   c   d   e

mountain   flat   wet

cross-training   food/water

notes: _____
_____
_____

Sunday

date   time   mileage

average speed   course   grade your ride

road   hilly   dry

       a   b   c   d   e

mountain   flat   wet

cross-training   food/water

notes: _____
_____
_____

Summary

weekly mileage   year to date

notes: _____
_____
_____
_____

Forget horns, bells, and whistles as warning devices. A loud scream originating deep in your diaphragm is instant and requires no hands.

Monday

date   time   mileage

average speed   course   grade your ride

    road hilly dry

              a b c d e

    mountain flat wet

  cross-training   food/water

notes: _____

_____

_____

Tuesday

date   time   mileage

average speed   course   grade your ride

    road hilly dry

              a b c d e

    mountain flat wet

  cross-training   food/water

notes: _____

_____

_____

Wednesday

date   time   mileage

average speed   course   grade your ride

    road hilly dry

              a b c d e

    mountain flat wet

  cross-training   food/water

notes: _____

_____

_____

Thursday

date   time   mileage

average speed   course   grade your ride

    road hilly dry

              a b c d e

    mountain flat wet

  cross-training   food/water

notes: _____

_____

_____

Friday

date   time   mileage

average speed   course   grade your ride

road   hilly   dry

mountain   flat   wet   a   b   c   d   e

cross-training   food/water

notes: _____

_____

_____

Saturday

date   time   mileage

average speed   course   grade your ride

road   hilly   dry

mountain   flat   wet   a   b   c   d   e

cross-training   food/water

notes: _____

_____

_____

Sunday

date   time   mileage

average speed   course   grade your ride

road   hilly   dry

mountain   flat   wet   a   b   c   d   e

cross-training   food/water

notes: _____

_____

_____

Summary

weekly mileage   year to date

notes: _____

_____

_____

_____

Never overlap the rear wheel of another rider. If he should veer and strike your front wheel, even lightly, you're likely to crash.

Monday
date   time   mileage

average speed   course   grade your ride

road hilly dry

               a b c d e

mountain flat wet

cross-training   food/water

notes: _____
_____
_____

Tuesday
date   time   mileage

average speed   course   grade your ride

road hilly dry

               a b c d e

mountain flat wet

cross-training   food/water

notes: _____
_____
_____

Wednesday
date   time   mileage

average speed   course   grade your ride

road hilly dry

               a b c d e

mountain flat wet

cross-training   food/water

notes: _____
_____
_____

Thursday
date   time   mileage

average speed   course   grade your ride

road hilly dry

               a b c d e

mountain flat wet

cross-training   food/water

notes: _____
_____
_____

Friday

date time mileage

average speed course grade your ride

road hilly dry

a b c d e

mountain flat wet

cross-training food/water

notes: _____

_____

_____

Saturday

date time mileage

average speed course grade your ride

road hilly dry

a b c d e

mountain flat wet

cross-training food/water

notes: _____

_____

_____

Sunday

date time mileage

average speed course grade your ride

road hilly dry

a b c d e

mountain flat wet

cross-training food/water

notes: _____

_____

_____

Summary

weekly mileage year to date

notes: _____

_____

_____

_____

Silence annoying clicks and creaks in clipless pedals by applying a few drops of oil to each shoe's cleat where it contacts the sole and to the pedal-gripping hardware.

Monday

date   time   mileage

average speed   course   grade your ride

road hilly dry

a b c d e

mountain flat wet

cross-training   food/water

notes: _____

_____

_____

Tuesday

date   time   mileage

average speed   course   grade your ride

road hilly dry

a b c d e

mountain flat wet

cross-training   food/water

notes: _____

_____

_____

Wednesday

date   time   mileage

average speed   course   grade your ride

road hilly dry

a b c d e

mountain flat wet

cross-training   food/water

notes: _____

_____

_____

Thursday

date   time   mileage

average speed   course   grade your ride

road hilly dry

a b c d e

mountain flat wet

cross-training   food/water

notes: _____

_____

_____

Friday

date   time   mileage

average speed   course   grade your ride

road   hilly   dry

a   b   c   d   e

mountain   flat   wet

cross-training   food/water

notes: _____

_____

_____

Saturday

date   time   mileage

average speed   course   grade your ride

road   hilly   dry

a   b   c   d   e

mountain   flat   wet

cross-training   food/water

notes: _____

_____

_____

Sunday

date   time   mileage

average speed   course   grade your ride

road   hilly   dry

a   b   c   d   e

mountain   flat   wet

cross-training   food/water

notes: _____

_____

_____

Summary

weekly mileage   year to date

notes: _____

_____

_____

_____

When applying mountain bike brakes, use them both, but apply the front more firmly—especially on descents, since there is more weight on the front tire.

Monday

date   time   mileage

average speed   course   grade your ride

road   hilly   dry

a   b   c   d   e

mountain   flat   wet

cross-training   food/water

notes: _____

_____

_____

Tuesday

date   time   mileage

average speed   course   grade your ride

road   hilly   dry

a   b   c   d   e

mountain   flat   wet

cross-training   food/water

notes: _____

_____

_____

Wednesday

date   time   mileage

average speed   course   grade your ride

road   hilly   dry

a   b   c   d   e

mountain   flat   wet

cross-training   food/water

notes: _____

_____

_____

Thursday

date   time   mileage

average speed   course   grade your ride

road   hilly   dry

a   b   c   d   e

mountain   flat   wet

cross-training   food/water

notes: _____

_____

_____

Friday

date   time   mileage

average speed   course   grade your ride

road hilly dry

           a b c d e

mountain flat wet

cross-training   food/water

notes: _____

_____

_____

Saturday

date   time   mileage

average speed   course   grade your ride

road hilly dry

           a b c d e

mountain flat wet

cross-training   food/water

notes: _____

_____

_____

Sunday

date   time   mileage

average speed   course   grade your ride

road hilly dry

           a b c d e

mountain flat wet

cross-training   food/water

notes: _____

_____

_____

Summary

weekly mileage   year to date

notes: _____

_____

_____

_____

When taking the lead position in a paceline, don't accelerate. Maintain the same cadence as when drafting, so you don't cause gaps to open between the other riders.

Monday

date   time   mileage

average speed   course   grade your ride

road   hilly   dry

a   b   c   d   e

mountain   flat   wet

cross-training   food/water

notes: _____

_____

_____

Tuesday

date   time   mileage

average speed   course   grade your ride

road   hilly   dry

a   b   c   d   e

mountain   flat   wet

cross-training   food/water

notes: _____

_____

_____

Wednesday

date   time   mileage

average speed   course   grade your ride

road   hilly   dry

a   b   c   d   e

mountain   flat   wet

cross-training   food/water

notes: _____

_____

_____

Thursday

date   time   mileage

average speed   course   grade your ride

road   hilly   dry

a   b   c   d   e

mountain   flat   wet

cross-training   food/water

notes: _____

_____

_____

TRAINING LOG

Friday

date   time   mileage

average speed   course   grade your ride

road   hilly   dry

a   b   c   d   e

mountain   flat   wet

cross-training   food/water

notes: _____
_____
_____

Saturday

date   time   mileage

average speed   course   grade your ride

road   hilly   dry

a   b   c   d   e

mountain   flat   wet

cross-training   food/water

notes: _____
_____
_____

Sunday

date   time   mileage

average speed   course   grade your ride

road   hilly   dry

a   b   c   d   e

mountain   flat   wet

cross-training   food/water

notes: _____
_____
_____

Summary

weekly mileage   year to date

notes: _____
_____
_____
_____

When you start to tire, change your body position. Stand for a minute. Or sit if you're out of the saddle. Alter your hand location on the handlebar.

Monday

date   time   mileage

average speed   course   grade your ride

road   hilly   dry
                                              a   b   c   d   e
mountain   flat   wet

cross-training   food/water

notes: _____
_____
_____

Tuesday

date   time   mileage

average speed   course   grade your ride

road   hilly   dry
                                              a   b   c   d   e
mountain   flat   wet

cross-training   food/water

notes: _____
_____
_____

Wednesday

date   time   mileage

average speed   course   grade your ride

road   hilly   dry
                                              a   b   c   d   e
mountain   flat   wet

cross-training   food/water

notes: _____
_____
_____

Thursday

date   time   mileage

average speed   course   grade your ride

road   hilly   dry
                                              a   b   c   d   e
mountain   flat   wet

cross-training   food/water

notes: _____
_____
_____

TRAINING LOG

Friday

date   time   mileage

average speed   course   grade your ride

road   hilly   dry

a   b   c   d   e

mountain   flat   wet

cross-training   food/water

notes: _____

_____

_____

Saturday

date   time   mileage

average speed   course   grade your ride

road   hilly   dry

a   b   c   d   e

mountain   flat   wet

cross-training   food/water

notes: _____

_____

_____

Sunday

date   time   mileage

average speed   course   grade your ride

road   hilly   dry

a   b   c   d   e

mountain   flat   wet

cross-training   food/water

notes: _____

_____

_____

Summary

weekly mileage   year to date

notes: _____

_____

_____

_____

Don't daydream. Always be aware of what's happening around you, whether in a race, on a group ride, or in traffic.

Monday

date   time   mileage

average speed   course   grade your ride

road   hilly   dry

a   b   c   d   e

mountain   flat   wet

cross-training   food/water

notes: _____

_____

_____

Tuesday

date   time   mileage

average speed   course   grade your ride

road   hilly   dry

a   b   c   d   e

mountain   flat   wet

cross-training   food/water

notes: _____

_____

_____

Wednesday

date   time   mileage

average speed   course   grade your ride

road   hilly   dry

a   b   c   d   e

mountain   flat   wet

cross-training   food/water

notes: _____

_____

_____

Thursday

date   time   mileage

average speed   course   grade your ride

road   hilly   dry

a   b   c   d   e

mountain   flat   wet

cross-training   food/water

notes: _____

_____

_____

Friday

date   time   mileage

average speed   course   grade your ride

road   hilly   dry

                                      a   b   c   d   e

mountain   flat   wet

cross-training   food/water

notes: _____

_____

_____

Saturday

date   time   mileage

average speed   course   grade your ride

road   hilly   dry

                                      a   b   c   d   e

mountain   flat   wet

cross-training   food/water

notes: _____

_____

_____

Sunday

date   time   mileage

average speed   course   grade your ride

road   hilly   dry

                                      a   b   c   d   e

mountain   flat   wet

cross-training   food/water

notes: _____

_____

_____

Summary

weekly mileage   year to date

notes: _____

_____

_____

_____

Memorize or record the distance from the center of your crankarm axle to the top of your saddle—it's handy when traveling or borrowing a bike.

Monday

date   time   mileage

average speed   course   grade your ride

road   hilly   dry

    a   b   c   d   e

mountain   flat   wet

cross-training   food/water

notes: _____

_____

_____

Tuesday

date   time   mileage

average speed   course   grade your ride

road   hilly   dry

    a   b   c   d   e

mountain   flat   wet

cross-training   food/water

notes: _____

_____

_____

Wednesday

date   time   mileage

average speed   course   grade your ride

road   hilly   dry

    a   b   c   d   e

mountain   flat   wet

cross-training   food/water

notes: _____

_____

_____

Thursday

date   time   mileage

average speed   course   grade your ride

road   hilly   dry

    a   b   c   d   e

mountain   flat   wet

cross-training   food/water

notes: _____

_____

_____

Friday

date   time   mileage

average speed   course   grade your ride

road   hilly   dry

a   b   c   d   e

mountain   flat   wet

cross-training   food/water

notes: _____
_____
_____

Saturday

date   time   mileage

average speed   course   grade your ride

road   hilly   dry

a   b   c   d   e

mountain   flat   wet

cross-training   food/water

notes: _____
_____
_____

Sunday

date   time   mileage

average speed   course   grade your ride

road   hilly   dry

a   b   c   d   e

mountain   flat   wet

cross-training   food/water

notes: _____
_____
_____

Summary

weekly mileage   year to date

notes: _____
_____
_____
_____

Stretching on the bike also helps minimize fatigue. Coast, put your left foot down, then lean far to the right to stretch your back and your left leg. Then do your right side.

Monday

date   time   mileage

average speed   course   grade your ride

road   hilly   dry

a   b   c   d   e

mountain   flat   wet

cross-training   food/water

notes: _____

_____

_____

Tuesday

date   time   mileage

average speed   course   grade your ride

road   hilly   dry

a   b   c   d   e

mountain   flat   wet

cross-training   food/water

notes: _____

_____

_____

Wednesday

date   time   mileage

average speed   course   grade your ride

road   hilly   dry

a   b   c   d   e

mountain   flat   wet

cross-training   food/water

notes: _____

_____

_____

Thursday

date   time   mileage

average speed   course   grade your ride

road   hilly   dry

a   b   c   d   e

mountain   flat   wet

cross-training   food/water

notes: _____

_____

_____

Friday

date   time   mileage

average speed   course   grade your ride

road   hilly   dry

a   b   c   d   e

mountain   flat   wet

cross-training   food/water

notes: _____

_____

_____

Saturday

date   time   mileage

average speed   course   grade your ride

road   hilly   dry

a   b   c   d   e

mountain   flat   wet

cross-training   food/water

notes: _____

_____

_____

Sunday

date   time   mileage

average speed   course   grade your ride

road   hilly   dry

a   b   c   d   e

mountain   flat   wet

cross-training   food/water

notes: _____

_____

_____

Summary

weekly mileage   year to date

notes: _____

_____

_____

_____

Coat your mountain bike's chain with a thick, gooey lubricant to protect it in wet, muddy conditions. Coat the entire drivetrain with a nonstick vegetable cooking spray.

Monday

date   time   mileage

average speed   course   grade your ride

road   hilly   dry

a   b   c   d   e

mountain   flat   wet

cross-training   food/water

notes: _____

_____

_____

Tuesday

date   time   mileage

average speed   course   grade your ride

road   hilly   dry

a   b   c   d   e

mountain   flat   wet

cross-training   food/water

notes: _____

_____

_____

Wednesday

date   time   mileage

average speed   course   grade your ride

road   hilly   dry

a   b   c   d   e

mountain   flat   wet

cross-training   food/water

notes: _____

_____

_____

Thursday

date   time   mileage

average speed   course   grade your ride

road   hilly   dry

a   b   c   d   e

mountain   flat   wet

cross-training   food/water

notes: _____

_____

_____

Friday

date   time   mileage

average speed   course   grade your ride

road   hilly   dry

a   b   c   d   e

mountain   flat   wet

cross-training   food/water

notes: _____

_____

_____

Saturday

date   time   mileage

average speed   course   grade your ride

road   hilly   dry

a   b   c   d   e

mountain   flat   wet

cross-training   food/water

notes: _____

_____

_____

Sunday

date   time   mileage

average speed   course   grade your ride

road   hilly   dry

a   b   c   d   e

mountain   flat   wet

cross-training   food/water

notes: _____

_____

_____

Summary

weekly mileage   year to date

notes: _____

_____

_____

_____

To get safely through a gravel-strewn corner, straighten up the bike until you're past the loose stuff, then resume turning. Avoid leaning the bike while on a gravelly or sandy surface.

Monday

date   time   mileage

average speed   course   grade your ride

road   hilly   dry

a   b   c   d   e

mountain   flat   wet

cross-training   food/water

notes: _____

_____

_____

Tuesday

date   time   mileage

average speed   course   grade your ride

road   hilly   dry

a   b   c   d   e

mountain   flat   wet

cross-training   food/water

notes: _____

_____

_____

Wednesday

date   time   mileage

average speed   course   grade your ride

road   hilly   dry

a   b   c   d   e

mountain   flat   wet

cross-training   food/water

notes: _____

_____

_____

Thursday

date   time   mileage

average speed   course   grade your ride

road   hilly   dry

a   b   c   d   e

mountain   flat   wet

cross-training   food/water

notes: _____

_____

_____

Friday

date   time   mileage

average speed   course   grade your ride
              road   hilly   dry
                                          a   b   c   d   e
              mountain   flat   wet
        cross-training   food/water

notes: _____
_____
_____

Saturday

date   time   mileage

average speed   course   grade your ride
              road   hilly   dry
                                          a   b   c   d   e
              mountain   flat   wet
        cross-training   food/water

notes: _____
_____
_____

Sunday

date   time   mileage

average speed   course   grade your ride
              road   hilly   dry
                                          a   b   c   d   e
              mountain   flat   wet
        cross-training   food/water

notes: _____
_____
_____

Summary

weekly mileage   year to date

notes: _____
_____
_____
_____

To loft the front wheel of your mountain bike over a bump, simultaneously lower your torso, apply a hard pedal stroke, and lift your arms. Shifting your weight forward will make the rear wheel bounce over lightly.

TRAINING LOG

Monday

date time mileage

average speed course grade your ride

road hilly dry

mountain flat wet

a b c d e

cross-training food/water

notes: _____
_____
_____

Tuesday

date time mileage

average speed course grade your ride

road hilly dry

mountain flat wet

a b c d e

cross-training food/water

notes: _____
_____
_____

Wednesday

date time mileage

average speed course grade your ride

road hilly dry

mountain flat wet

a b c d e

cross-training food/water

notes: _____
_____
_____

Thursday

date time mileage

average speed course grade your ride

road hilly dry

mountain flat wet

a b c d e

cross-training food/water

notes: _____
_____
_____

Friday

date   time   mileage

average speed   course   grade your ride

road   hilly   dry

a b c d e

mountain flat wet

cross-training   food/water

notes: _____
_____
_____

Saturday

date   time   mileage

average speed   course   grade your ride

road   hilly   dry

a b c d e

mountain flat wet

cross-training   food/water

notes: _____
_____
_____

Sunday

date   time   mileage

average speed   course   grade your ride

road   hilly   dry

a b c d e

mountain flat wet

cross-training   food/water

notes: _____
_____
_____

Summary

weekly mileage   year to date

notes: _____
_____
_____
_____

Communication is the key to safe group rides. Make sure that everyone knows of approaching turns, stops, and hazards by calling them out.

Monday

date   time   mileage

average speed   course   grade your ride

road   hilly   dry

            a   b   c   d   e

mountain   flat   wet

cross-training   food/water

notes: _____

_____

_____

Tuesday

date   time   mileage

average speed   course   grade your ride

road   hilly   dry

            a   b   c   d   e

mountain   flat   wet

cross-training   food/water

notes: _____

_____

_____

Wednesday

date   time   mileage

average speed   course   grade your ride

road   hilly   dry

            a   b   c   d   e

mountain   flat   wet

cross-training   food/water

notes: _____

_____

_____

Thursday

date   time   mileage

average speed   course   grade your ride

road   hilly   dry

            a   b   c   d   e

mountain   flat   wet

cross-training   food/water

notes: _____

_____

_____

Friday

date   time   mileage

average speed   course   grade your ride

    road   hilly   dry

                 a   b   c   d   e

    mountain   flat   wet

cross-training   food/water

notes: _____
_____
_____

Saturday

date   time   mileage

average speed   course   grade your ride

    road   hilly   dry

                 a   b   c   d   e

    mountain   flat   wet

cross-training   food/water

notes: _____
_____
_____

Sunday

date   time   mileage

average speed   course   grade your ride

    road   hilly   dry

                 a   b   c   d   e

    mountain   flat   wet

cross-training   food/water

notes: _____
_____
_____

Summary

weekly mileage   year to date

notes: _____
_____
_____
_____

When what lies ahead is a boggy mess of mud, momentum is the key. Stay in the saddle and keep pedaling to maintain balance and forward progress.

Monday

date   time   mileage

average speed   course   grade your ride

road   hilly   dry

a   b   c   d   e

mountain   flat   wet

cross-training   food/water

notes: _____
_____
_____

Tuesday

date   time   mileage

average speed   course   grade your ride

road   hilly   dry

a   b   c   d   e

mountain   flat   wet

cross-training   food/water

notes: _____
_____
_____

Wednesday

date   time   mileage

average speed   course   grade your ride

road   hilly   dry

a   b   c   d   e

mountain   flat   wet

cross-training   food/water

notes: _____
_____
_____

Thursday

date   time   mileage

average speed   course   grade your ride

road   hilly   dry

a   b   c   d   e

mountain   flat   wet

cross-training   food/water

notes: _____
_____
_____

Friday

date   time   mileage

average speed   course   grade your ride

road   hilly   dry

a b c d e

mountain flat wet

cross-training   food/water

notes: _____

_____

_____

Saturday

date   time   mileage

average speed   course   grade your ride

road   hilly   dry

a b c d e

mountain flat wet

cross-training   food/water

notes: _____

_____

_____

Sunday

date   time   mileage

average speed   course   grade your ride

road   hilly   dry

a b c d e

mountain flat wet

cross-training   food/water

notes: _____

_____

_____

Summary

weekly mileage   year to date

notes: _____

_____

_____

_____

Don't grasp the handlebar drops when climbing, because it compresses the diaphragm and inhibits breathing. Instead, use the bar top.

Monday
date   time   mileage

average speed   course   grade your ride

road   hilly   dry

a   b   c   d   e

mountain   flat   wet

cross-training   food/water

notes: _____
_____
_____

Tuesday
date   time   mileage

average speed   course   grade your ride

road   hilly   dry

a   b   c   d   e

mountain   flat   wet

cross-training   food/water

notes: _____
_____
_____

Wednesday
date   time   mileage

average speed   course   grade your ride

road   hilly   dry

a   b   c   d   e

mountain   flat   wet

cross-training   food/water

notes: _____
_____
_____

Thursday
date   time   mileage

average speed   course   grade your ride

road   hilly   dry

a   b   c   d   e

mountain   flat   wet

cross-training   food/water

notes: _____
_____
_____

Friday

date   time   mileage

average speed   course   grade your ride

road   hilly   dry

a   b   c   d   e

mountain   flat   wet

cross-training   food/water

notes: _____

_____

_____

Saturday

date   time   mileage

average speed   course   grade your ride

road   hilly   dry

a   b   c   d   e

mountain   flat   wet

cross-training   food/water

notes: _____

_____

_____

Sunday

date   time   mileage

average speed   course   grade your ride

road   hilly   dry

a   b   c   d   e

mountain   flat   wet

cross-training   food/water

notes: _____

_____

_____

Summary

weekly mileage   year to date

notes: _____

_____

_____

_____

Because wind usually increases during the day, plan a morning ride so your route takes you into a gentle breeze that becomes a brisk tailwind on your return.

Monday

date   time   mileage

average speed   course   grade your ride

road   hilly   dry

     a   b   c   d   e

mountain   flat   wet

cross-training   food/water

notes: _____

_____

_____

Tuesday

date   time   mileage

average speed   course   grade your ride

road   hilly   dry

     a   b   c   d   e

mountain   flat   wet

cross-training   food/water

notes: _____

_____

_____

Wednesday

date   time   mileage

average speed   course   grade your ride

road   hilly   dry

     a   b   c   d   e

mountain   flat   wet

cross-training   food/water

notes: _____

_____

_____

Thursday

date   time   mileage

average speed   course   grade your ride

road   hilly   dry

     a   b   c   d   e

mountain   flat   wet

cross-training   food/water

notes: _____

_____

_____

Friday

date   time   mileage

average speed   course   grade your ride

road   hilly   dry

mountain   flat   wet

a   b   c   d   e

cross-training   food/water

notes: _____

_____

_____

Saturday

date   time   mileage

average speed   course   grade your ride

road   hilly   dry

mountain   flat   wet

a   b   c   d   e

cross-training   food/water

notes: _____

_____

_____

Sunday

date   time   mileage

average speed   course   grade your ride

road   hilly   dry

mountain   flat   wet

a   b   c   d   e

cross-training   food/water

notes: _____

_____

_____

Summary

weekly mileage   year to date

notes: _____

_____

_____

_____

As your effort becomes harder, increase the force of your breaths rather than their frequency.

Monday

date   time   mileage

average speed   course   grade your ride

road hilly dry

a b c d e

mountain flat wet

cross-training   food/water

notes: _____
_____
_____

Tuesday

date   time   mileage

average speed   course   grade your ride

road hilly dry

a b c d e

mountain flat wet

cross-training   food/water

notes: _____
_____
_____

Wednesday

date   time   mileage

average speed   course   grade your ride

road hilly dry

a b c d e

mountain flat wet

cross-training   food/water

notes: _____
_____
_____

Thursday

date   time   mileage

average speed   course   grade your ride

road hilly dry

a b c d e

mountain flat wet

cross-training   food/water

notes: _____
_____
_____

Friday

date	time	mileage

average speed

course

grade your ride

road   hilly   dry

a b c d e

mountain   flat   wet

cross-training   food/water

notes: _____

_____

_____

Saturday

date	time	mileage

average speed

course

grade your ride

road   hilly   dry

a b c d e

mountain   flat   wet

cross-training   food/water

notes: _____

_____

_____

Sunday

date	time	mileage

average speed

course

grade your ride

road   hilly   dry

a b c d e

mountain   flat   wet

cross-training   food/water

notes: _____

_____

_____

Summary

weekly mileage	year to date

notes: _____

_____

_____

_____

Beware of using a gas station's air pump. It delivers a large volume of air quickly and can blow a bike tire off the rim.

Monday

date   time   mileage

average speed   course   grade your ride

road   hilly   dry

a b c d e

mountain   flat   wet

cross-training   food/water

notes: _____

_____

_____

Tuesday

date   time   mileage

average speed   course   grade your ride

road   hilly   dry

a b c d e

mountain   flat   wet

cross-training   food/water

notes: _____

_____

_____

Wednesday

date   time   mileage

average speed   course   grade your ride

road   hilly   dry

a b c d e

mountain   flat   wet

cross-training   food/water

notes: _____

_____

_____

Thursday

date   time   mileage

average speed   course   grade your ride

road   hilly   dry

a b c d e

mountain   flat   wet

cross-training   food/water

notes: _____

_____

_____

Friday

date   time   mileage

average speed   course   grade your ride

          road   hilly   dry

               a   b   c   d   e

          mountain   flat   wet

cross-training   food/water

notes: _____

_____

_____

Saturday

date   time   mileage

average speed   course   grade your ride

          road   hilly   dry

               a   b   c   d   e

          mountain   flat   wet

cross-training   food/water

notes: _____

_____

_____

Sunday

date   time   mileage

average speed   course   grade your ride

          road   hilly   dry

               a   b   c   d   e

          mountain   flat   wet

cross-training   food/water

notes: _____

_____

_____

Summary

weekly mileage   year to date

notes: _____

_____

_____

_____

To jump a wide object, such as a set of railroad tracks, keep your speed up. If you hesitate and then decide to jump, only the front wheel will make it across.

Monday

date   time   mileage

average speed   course   grade your ride

road   hilly   dry

a b c d e

mountain   flat   wet

cross-training   food/water

notes: _____

_____

_____

Tuesday

date   time   mileage

average speed   course   grade your ride

road   hilly   dry

a b c d e

mountain   flat   wet

cross-training   food/water

notes: _____

_____

_____

Wednesday

date   time   mileage

average speed   course   grade your ride

road   hilly   dry

a b c d e

mountain   flat   wet

cross-training   food/water

notes: _____

_____

_____

Thursday

date   time   mileage

average speed   course   grade your ride

road   hilly   dry

a b c d e

mountain   flat   wet

cross-training   food/water

notes: _____

_____

_____

Friday

date   time   mileage

average speed   course   grade your ride

road   hilly   dry

a   b   c   d   e

mountain   flat   wet

cross-training   food/water

notes: _____

_____

_____

Saturday

date   time   mileage

average speed   course   grade your ride

road   hilly   dry

a   b   c   d   e

mountain   flat   wet

cross-training   food/water

notes: _____

_____

_____

Sunday

date   time   mileage

average speed   course   grade your ride

road   hilly   dry

a   b   c   d   e

mountain   flat   wet

cross-training   food/water

notes: _____

_____

_____

Summary

weekly mileage   year to date

notes: _____

_____

_____

_____

During long descents on wet roads, maintain slight brake pad contact with the rims to keep them free of excess water and allow quicker stopping.

Monday

date   time   mileage

average speed   course   grade your ride

road   hilly   dry

a   b   c   d   e

mountain   flat   wet

cross-training   food/water

notes: _____
_____
_____

Tuesday

date   time   mileage

average speed   course   grade your ride

road   hilly   dry

a   b   c   d   e

mountain   flat   wet

cross-training   food/water

notes: _____
_____
_____

Wednesday

date   time   mileage

average speed   course   grade your ride

road   hilly   dry

a   b   c   d   e

mountain   flat   wet

cross-training   food/water

notes: _____
_____
_____

Thursday

date   time   mileage

average speed   course   grade your ride

road   hilly   dry

a   b   c   d   e

mountain   flat   wet

cross-training   food/water

notes: _____
_____
_____

Friday

date   time   mileage

average speed   course   grade your ride

road   hilly   dry

a   b   c   d   e

mountain   flat   wet

cross-training   food/water

notes: _____
_____
_____

Saturday

date   time   mileage

average speed   course   grade your ride

road   hilly   dry

a   b   c   d   e

mountain   flat   wet

cross-training   food/water

notes: _____
_____
_____

Sunday

date   time   mileage

average speed   course   grade your ride

road   hilly   dry

a   b   c   d   e

mountain   flat   wet

cross-training   food/water

notes: _____
_____
_____

Summary

weekly mileage   year to date

notes: _____
_____
_____
_____

Whatever type of lock you use, don't place it near the ground. In that position, it's easier for a thief to apply leverage with tools or crush it with a hammer.

Monday

date   time   mileage

average speed   course   grade your ride

road   hilly   dry

a   b   c   d   e

mountain   flat   wet

cross-training   food/water

notes: _____

_____

_____

Tuesday

date   time   mileage

average speed   course   grade your ride

road   hilly   dry

a   b   c   d   e

mountain   flat   wet

cross-training   food/water

notes: _____

_____

_____

Wednesday

date   time   mileage

average speed   course   grade your ride

road   hilly   dry

a   b   c   d   e

mountain   flat   wet

cross-training   food/water

notes: _____

_____

_____

Thursday

date   time   mileage

average speed   course   grade your ride

road   hilly   dry

a   b   c   d   e

mountain   flat   wet

cross-training   food/water

notes: _____

_____

_____

Friday

date   time   mileage

average speed   course   grade your ride

road   hilly   dry

        a   b   c   d   e

mountain   flat   wet

cross-training   food/water

notes: _____
_____
_____

Saturday

date   time   mileage

average speed   course   grade your ride

road   hilly   dry

        a   b   c   d   e

mountain   flat   wet

cross-training   food/water

notes: _____
_____
_____

Sunday

date   time   mileage

average speed   course   grade your ride

road   hilly   dry

        a   b   c   d   e

mountain   flat   wet

cross-training   food/water

notes: _____
_____
_____

Summary

weekly mileage   year to date

notes: _____
_____
_____
_____

Use the whole saddle during rides. Sit in the center for normal pedaling, scoot forward to increase your spin, and slide back to power up a hill.

Monday

date   time   mileage

average speed   course   grade your ride

road   hilly   dry

a   b   c   d   e

mountain   flat   wet

cross-training   food/water

notes: _____

_____

_____

Tuesday

date   time   mileage

average speed   course   grade your ride

road   hilly   dry

a   b   c   d   e

mountain   flat   wet

cross-training   food/water

notes: _____

_____

_____

Wednesday

date   time   mileage

average speed   course   grade your ride

road   hilly   dry

a   b   c   d   e

mountain   flat   wet

cross-training   food/water

notes: _____

_____

_____

Thursday

date   time   mileage

average speed   course   grade your ride

road   hilly   dry

a   b   c   d   e

mountain   flat   wet

cross-training   food/water

notes: _____

_____

_____

Friday
date   time   mileage

average speed   course   grade your ride

road   hilly   dry   a   b   c   d   e

mountain   flat   wet

cross-training   food/water

notes: _____

_____

_____

Saturday
date   time   mileage

average speed   course   grade your ride

road   hilly   dry   a   b   c   d   e

mountain   flat   wet

cross-training   food/water

notes: _____

_____

_____

Sunday
date   time   mileage

average speed   course   grade your ride

road   hilly   dry   a   b   c   d   e

mountain   flat   wet

cross-training   food/water

notes: _____

_____

_____

Summary
weekly mileage   year to date

notes: _____

_____

_____

_____

The best way to recover from a hard effort is to ride easily the next day rather than take the day off. Use the opportunity to cycle with family and friends.

Monday

date   time   mileage

average speed   course   grade your ride

road   hilly   dry

a   b   c   d   e

mountain   flat   wet

cross-training   food/water

notes: _____

_____

_____

Tuesday

date   time   mileage

average speed   course   grade your ride

road   hilly   dry

a   b   c   d   e

mountain   flat   wet

cross-training   food/water

notes: _____

_____

_____

Wednesday

date   time   mileage

average speed   course   grade your ride

road   hilly   dry

a   b   c   d   e

mountain   flat   wet

cross-training   food/water

notes: _____

_____

_____

Thursday

date   time   mileage

average speed   course   grade your ride

road   hilly   dry

a   b   c   d   e

mountain   flat   wet

cross-training   food/water

notes: _____

_____

_____

Friday

date   time   mileage

average speed   course   grade your ride

road   hilly   dry

a   b   c   d   e

mountain   flat   wet

cross-training   food/water

notes: _____

_____

_____

Saturday

date   time   mileage

average speed   course   grade your ride

road   hilly   dry

a   b   c   d   e

mountain   flat   wet

cross-training   food/water

notes: _____

_____

_____

Sunday

date   time   mileage

average speed   course   grade your ride

road   hilly   dry

a   b   c   d   e

mountain   flat   wet

cross-training   food/water

notes: _____

_____

_____

Summary

weekly mileage   year to date

notes: _____

_____

_____

_____

The key to building muscle strength for cycling is to perform numerous repetitions with light to moderate weights. This will also increase your muscle endurance without adding bulk.

Monday

date   time   mileage

average speed   course   grade your ride

     road   hilly   dry

               a   b   c   d   e

     mountain   flat   wet

cross-training   food/water

notes: _____

_____

_____

Tuesday

date   time   mileage

average speed   course   grade your ride

     road   hilly   dry

               a   b   c   d   e

     mountain   flat   wet

cross-training   food/water

notes: _____

_____

_____

Wednesday

date   time   mileage

average speed   course   grade your ride

     road   hilly   dry

               a   b   c   d   e

     mountain   flat   wet

cross-training   food/water

notes: _____

_____

_____

Thursday

date   time   mileage

average speed   course   grade your ride

     road   hilly   dry

               a   b   c   d   e

     mountain   flat   wet

cross-training   food/water

notes: _____

_____

_____

Friday

date   time   mileage

average speed   course   grade your ride

road   hilly   dry

            a   b   c   d   e

mountain   flat   wet

cross-training   food/water

notes: _____

_____

_____

Saturday

date   time   mileage

average speed   course   grade your ride

road   hilly   dry

            a   b   c   d   e

mountain   flat   wet

cross-training   food/water

notes: _____

_____

_____

Sunday

date   time   mileage

average speed   course   grade your ride

road   hilly   dry

            a   b   c   d   e

mountain   flat   wet

cross-training   food/water

notes: _____

_____

_____

Summary

weekly mileage   year to date

notes: _____

_____

_____

_____

If you need to rest before a race, do so two days before. Take a short ride on the eve of the event, and include a couple of sprints to make sure that your bike and body are operating well.

Monday

date   time   mileage

average speed   course   grade your ride

road   hilly   dry

    a   b   c   d   e

mountain   flat   wet

cross-training   food/water

notes: _____

_____

_____

Tuesday

date   time   mileage

average speed   course   grade your ride

road   hilly   dry

    a   b   c   d   e

mountain   flat   wet

cross-training   food/water

notes: _____

_____

_____

Wednesday

date   time   mileage

average speed   course   grade your ride

road   hilly   dry

    a   b   c   d   e

mountain   flat   wet

cross-training   food/water

notes: _____

_____

_____

Thursday

date   time   mileage

average speed   course   grade your ride

road   hilly   dry

    a   b   c   d   e

mountain   flat   wet

cross-training   food/water

notes: _____

_____

_____

Friday

date   time   mileage

average speed   course   grade your ride

road   hilly   dry

     a   b   c   d   e

mountain   flat   wet

cross-training   food/water

notes: _____

_____

_____

Saturday

date   time   mileage

average speed   course   grade your ride

road   hilly   dry

     a   b   c   d   e

mountain   flat   wet

cross-training   food/water

notes: _____

_____

_____

Sunday

date   time   mileage

average speed   course   grade your ride

road   hilly   dry

     a   b   c   d   e

mountain   flat   wet

cross-training   food/water

notes: _____

_____

_____

Summary

weekly mileage   year to date

notes: _____

_____

_____

_____

Use this order of adjustments to make a bike of proper size fit your body perfectly: cleat position, saddle tilt, saddle height, knee-over-pedal relationship, reach to handlebar.

Monday

date   time   mileage

average speed   course   grade your ride

         road   hilly   dry

                           a   b   c   d   e

         mountain   flat   wet

cross-training   food/water

notes: _____

_____

_____

Tuesday

date   time   mileage

average speed   course   grade your ride

         road   hilly   dry

                           a   b   c   d   e

         mountain   flat   wet

cross-training   food/water

notes: _____

_____

_____

Wednesday

date   time   mileage

average speed   course   grade your ride

         road   hilly   dry

                           a   b   c   d   e

         mountain   flat   wet

cross-training   food/water

notes: _____

_____

_____

Thursday

date   time   mileage

average speed   course   grade your ride

         road   hilly   dry

                           a   b   c   d   e

         mountain   flat   wet

cross-training   food/water

notes: _____

_____

_____

Friday

date	time	mileage

average speed   course   grade your ride

    road   hilly   dry

                            a   b   c   d   e

    mountain   flat   wet

cross-training   food/water

notes: _____

_____

_____

Saturday

date	time	mileage

average speed   course   grade your ride

    road   hilly   dry

                            a   b   c   d   e

    mountain   flat   wet

cross-training   food/water

notes: _____

_____

_____

Sunday

date	time	mileage

average speed   course   grade your ride

    road   hilly   dry

                            a   b   c   d   e

    mountain   flat   wet

cross-training   food/water

notes: _____

_____

_____

Summary

weekly mileage	year to date

notes: _____

_____

_____

_____

To facilitate breathing, make sure that the width of your handlebar equals the width of your shoulders.

Monday

date   time   mileage

average speed   course   grade your ride

road   hilly   dry

a   b   c   d   e

mountain   flat   wet

cross-training   food/water

notes: _____

_____

_____

Tuesday

date   time   mileage

average speed   course   grade your ride

road   hilly   dry

a   b   c   d   e

mountain   flat   wet

cross-training   food/water

notes: _____

_____

_____

Wednesday

date   time   mileage

average speed   course   grade your ride

road   hilly   dry

a   b   c   d   e

mountain   flat   wet

cross-training   food/water

notes: _____

_____

_____

Thursday

date   time   mileage

average speed   course   grade your ride

road   hilly   dry

a   b   c   d   e

mountain   flat   wet

cross-training   food/water

notes: _____

_____

_____

Friday

date   time   mileage

average speed   course   grade your ride

      road   hilly   dry

                            a   b   c   d   e

      mountain   flat   wet

cross-training   food/water

notes: _____

_____

_____

Saturday

date   time   mileage

average speed   course   grade your ride

      road   hilly   dry

                            a   b   c   d   e

      mountain   flat   wet

cross-training   food/water

notes: _____

_____

_____

Sunday

date   time   mileage

average speed   course   grade your ride

      road   hilly   dry

                            a   b   c   d   e

      mountain   flat   wet

cross-training   food/water

notes: _____

_____

_____

Summary

weekly mileage   year to date

notes: _____

_____

_____

_____

Opt for a smaller frame on a mountain bike if you're unsure about the exact size to ride. More top-tube clearance can't hurt when you have to hop off to prevent a fall.

TRAINING LOG

Monday

date   time   mileage

average speed   course   grade your ride

road   hilly   dry

a   b   c   d   e

mountain   flat   wet

cross-training   food/water

notes: _____

_____

_____

Tuesday

date   time   mileage

average speed   course   grade your ride

road   hilly   dry

a   b   c   d   e

mountain   flat   wet

cross-training   food/water

notes: _____

_____

_____

Wednesday

date   time   mileage

average speed   course   grade your ride

road   hilly   dry

a   b   c   d   e

mountain   flat   wet

cross-training   food/water

notes: _____

_____

_____

Thursday

date   time   mileage

average speed   course   grade your ride

road   hilly   dry

a   b   c   d   e

mountain   flat   wet

cross-training   food/water

notes: _____

_____

_____

Friday

date   time   mileage

average speed   course   grade your ride

road   hilly   dry

     a   b   c   d   e

mountain   flat   wet

cross-training   food/water

notes: _____
_____
_____

Saturday

date   time   mileage

average speed   course   grade your ride

road   hilly   dry

     a   b   c   d   e

mountain   flat   wet

cross-training   food/water

notes: _____
_____
_____

Sunday

date   time   mileage

average speed   course   grade your ride

road   hilly   dry

     a   b   c   d   e

mountain   flat   wet

cross-training   food/water

notes: _____
_____
_____

Summary

weekly mileage   year to date

notes: _____
_____
_____
_____

The two surest and easiest ways to help your bike work well are to maintain proper tire pressure and frequently lubricate your chain.

Monday

date　　　time　　　mileage

average speed　　　　course　　　　grade your ride

road　　hilly　　dry

　　　　　　　　　　　　　　　　　　a　b　c　d　e

mountain　flat　　wet

cross-training　　　　　　　food/water

notes: _____

_____

_____

Tuesday

date　　　time　　　mileage

average speed　　　　course　　　　grade your ride

road　　hilly　　dry

　　　　　　　　　　　　　　　　　　a　b　c　d　e

mountain　flat　　wet

cross-training　　　　　　　food/water

notes: _____

_____

_____

Wednesday

date　　　time　　　mileage

average speed　　　　course　　　　grade your ride

road　　hilly　　dry

　　　　　　　　　　　　　　　　　　a　b　c　d　e

mountain　flat　　wet

cross-training　　　　　　　food/water

notes: _____

_____

_____

Thursday

date　　　time　　　mileage

average speed　　　　course　　　　grade your ride

road　　hilly　　dry

　　　　　　　　　　　　　　　　　　a　b　c　d　e

mountain　flat　　wet

cross-training　　　　　　　food/water

notes: _____

_____

_____

TRAINING LOG

Friday

date   time   mileage

average speed   course   grade your ride

road   hilly   dry

     a   b   c   d   e

mountain   flat   wet

cross-training   food/water

notes: _____
_____
_____

Saturday

date   time   mileage

average speed   course   grade your ride

road   hilly   dry

     a   b   c   d   e

mountain   flat   wet

cross-training   food/water

notes: _____
_____
_____

Sunday

date   time   mileage

average speed   course   grade your ride

road   hilly   dry

     a   b   c   d   e

mountain   flat   wet

cross-training   food/water

notes: _____
_____
_____

Summary

weekly mileage   year to date

notes: _____
_____
_____
_____

To improve your chances of making it safely through a fast turn, keep your center of gravity low by staying down on the bike and pointing your inside knee into the turn.

Monday

date   time   mileage

average speed   course   grade your ride

road   hilly   dry

a   b   c   d   e

mountain   flat   wet

cross-training   food/water

notes: _____

_____

_____

Tuesday

date   time   mileage

average speed   course   grade your ride

road   hilly   dry

a   b   c   d   e

mountain   flat   wet

cross-training   food/water

notes: _____

_____

_____

Wednesday

date   time   mileage

average speed   course   grade your ride

road   hilly   dry

a   b   c   d   e

mountain   flat   wet

cross-training   food/water

notes: _____

_____

_____

Thursday

date   time   mileage

average speed   course   grade your ride

road   hilly   dry

a   b   c   d   e

mountain   flat   wet

cross-training   food/water

notes: _____

_____

_____

Friday

date   time   mileage

average speed   course   grade your ride

      road   hilly   dry

                                       a   b   c   d   e

      mountain   flat   wet

cross-training   food/water

notes: _____

_____

_____

Saturday

date   time   mileage

average speed   course   grade your ride

      road   hilly   dry

                                         a   b   c   d   e

      mountain   flat   wet

cross-training   food/water

notes: _____

_____

_____

Sunday

date   time   mileage

average speed   course   grade your ride

      road   hilly   dry

                                         a   b   c   d   e

      mountain   flat   wet

cross-training   food/water

notes: _____

_____

_____

Summary

weekly mileage   year to date

notes: _____

_____

_____

_____

Don't downshift too soon on a hill. It will steal your momentum and you'll have to work harder.

TRAINING LOG

Monday

date   time   mileage

average speed   course   grade your ride

road   hilly   dry

            a   b   c   d   e

mountain   flat   wet

cross-training   food/water

notes: _____

_____

_____

Tuesday

date   time   mileage

average speed   course   grade your ride

road   hilly   dry

            a   b   c   d   e

mountain   flat   wet

cross-training   food/water

notes: _____

_____

_____

Wednesday

date   time   mileage

average speed   course   grade your ride

road   hilly   dry

            a   b   c   d   e

mountain   flat   wet

cross-training   food/water

notes: _____

_____

_____

Thursday

date   time   mileage

average speed   course   grade your ride

road   hilly   dry

            a   b   c   d   e

mountain   flat   wet

cross-training   food/water

notes: _____

_____

_____

TRAINING LOG

Friday

date   time   mileage

average speed   course   grade your ride

road   hilly   dry

    a   b   c   d   e

mountain   flat   wet

cross-training   food/water

notes: _____

_____

_____

Saturday

date   time   mileage

average speed   course   grade your ride

road   hilly   dry

    a   b   c   d   e

mountain   flat   wet

cross-training   food/water

notes: _____

_____

_____

Sunday

date   time   mileage

average speed   course   grade your ride

road   hilly   dry

    a   b   c   d   e

mountain   flat   wet

cross-training   food/water

notes: _____

_____

_____

Summary

weekly mileage   year to date

notes: _____

_____

_____

_____

When mountain biking, look for changes in ground color. In dry climates, for instance, darker soil usually harbors more moisture and better traction.

Monday
date   time   mileage

average speed   course   grade your ride

road   hilly   dry

     a   b   c   d   e

mountain   flat   wet

cross-training   food/water

notes: _____
_____
_____

Tuesday
date   time   mileage

average speed   course   grade your ride

road   hilly   dry

     a   b   c   d   e

mountain   flat   wet

cross-training   food/water

notes: _____
_____
_____

Wednesday
date   time   mileage

average speed   course   grade your ride

road   hilly   dry

     a   b   c   d   e

mountain   flat   wet

cross-training   food/water

notes: _____
_____
_____

Thursday
date   time   mileage

average speed   course   grade your ride

road   hilly   dry

     a   b   c   d   e

mountain   flat   wet

cross-training   food/water

notes: _____
_____
_____

TRAINING LOG

Friday

date   time   mileage

average speed   course   grade your ride

road   hilly   dry

a   b   c   d   e

mountain   flat   wet

cross-training   food/water

notes: _____

_____

_____

Saturday

date   time   mileage

average speed   course   grade your ride

road   hilly   dry

a   b   c   d   e

mountain   flat   wet

cross-training   food/water

notes: _____

_____

_____

Sunday

date   time   mileage

average speed   course   grade your ride

road   hilly   dry

a   b   c   d   e

mountain   flat   wet

cross-training   food/water

notes: _____

_____

_____

Summary

weekly mileage   year to date

notes: _____

_____

_____

_____

Check the glue in your patch kit periodically to be sure that it hasn't evaporated.

Monday

date   time   mileage

average speed   course   grade your ride

road   hilly   dry

a b c d e

mountain   flat   wet

cross-training   food/water

notes: _____

_____

_____

Tuesday

date   time   mileage

average speed   course   grade your ride

road   hilly   dry

a b c d e

mountain   flat   wet

cross-training   food/water

notes: _____

_____

_____

Wednesday

date   time   mileage

average speed   course   grade your ride

road   hilly   dry

a b c d e

mountain   flat   wet

cross-training   food/water

notes: _____

_____

_____

Thursday

date   time   mileage

average speed   course   grade your ride

road   hilly   dry

a b c d e

mountain   flat   wet

cross-training   food/water

notes: _____

_____

_____

Friday

date   time   mileage

average speed

	course		grade your ride
road	hilly	dry	
			a b c d e
mountain	flat	wet	

cross-training   food/water

notes: _____
_____
_____

Saturday

date   time   mileage

average speed

	course		grade your ride
road	hilly	dry	
			a b c d e
mountain	flat	wet	

cross-training   food/water

notes: _____
_____
_____

Sunday

date   time   mileage

average speed

	course		grade your ride
road	hilly	dry	
			a b c d e
mountain	flat	wet	

cross-training   food/water

notes: _____
_____
_____

Summary

weekly mileage   year to date

notes: _____
_____
_____
_____

Write your name, address, phone number, and "This bike was stolen" on a piece of tape and stick it to the fork's steerer tube. Then if your bike is ever stolen, a shop mechanic may contact you.

Monday

date   time   mileage

average speed   course   grade your ride

road   hilly   dry

a   b   c   d   e

mountain   flat   wet

cross-training   food/water

notes: _____

_____

_____

Tuesday

date   time   mileage

average speed   course   grade your ride

road   hilly   dry

a   b   c   d   e

mountain   flat   wet

cross-training   food/water

notes: _____

_____

_____

Wednesday

date   time   mileage

average speed   course   grade your ride

road   hilly   dry

a   b   c   d   e

mountain   flat   wet

cross-training   food/water

notes: _____

_____

_____

Thursday

date   time   mileage

average speed   course   grade your ride

road   hilly   dry

a   b   c   d   e

mountain   flat   wet

cross-training   food/water

notes: _____

_____

_____

Friday

date   time   mileage

average speed   course   grade your ride

road   hilly   dry

a   b   c   d   e

mountain   flat   wet

cross-training   food/water

notes: _____
_____
_____

Saturday

date   time   mileage

average speed   course   grade your ride

road   hilly   dry

a   b   c   d   e

mountain   flat   wet

cross-training   food/water

notes: _____
_____
_____

Sunday

date   time   mileage

average speed   course   grade your ride

road   hilly   dry

a   b   c   d   e

mountain   flat   wet

cross-training   food/water

notes: _____
_____
_____

Summary

weekly mileage   year to date

notes: _____
_____
_____
_____

Never use a narrow tire on a wide rim. There isn't enough rubber to protect the metal from potholes and rocks.

Monday

date   time   mileage

average speed   course   grade your ride

road   hilly   dry

a   b   c   d   e

mountain   flat   wet

cross-training   food/water

notes: _____

_____

_____

Tuesday

date   time   mileage

average speed   course   grade your ride

road   hilly   dry

a   b   c   d   e

mountain   flat   wet

cross-training   food/water

notes: _____

_____

_____

Wednesday

date   time   mileage

average speed   course   grade your ride

road   hilly   dry

a   b   c   d   e

mountain   flat   wet

cross-training   food/water

notes: _____

_____

_____

Thursday

date   time   mileage

average speed   course   grade your ride

road   hilly   dry

a   b   c   d   e

mountain   flat   wet

cross-training   food/water

notes: _____

_____

_____

Friday

date   time   mileage

average speed   course   grade your ride

road   hilly   dry

       a   b   c   d   e

mountain   flat   wet

cross-training   food/water

notes: _____

_____

_____

Saturday

date   time   mileage

average speed   course   grade your ride

road   hilly   dry

       a   b   c   d   e

mountain   flat   wet

cross-training   food/water

notes: _____

_____

_____

Sunday

date   time   mileage

average speed   course   grade your ride

road   hilly   dry

       a   b   c   d   e

mountain   flat   wet

cross-training   food/water

notes: _____

_____

_____

Summary

weekly mileage   year to date

notes: _____

_____

_____

_____

To calculate cadence (pedal revolutions per minute), count the number of times your right foot reaches the bottom of the pedal stroke in 15 seconds, then multiply by four.

Monday

date   time   mileage

average speed   course   grade your ride
                    road   hilly   dry
                                                    a   b   c   d   e
                    mountain flat   wet
            cross-training   food/water

notes: _____
_____
_____

Tuesday

date   time   mileage

average speed   course   grade your ride
                    road   hilly   dry
                                                    a   b   c   d   e
                    mountain flat   wet
            cross-training   food/water

notes: _____
_____
_____

Wednesday

date   time   mileage

average speed   course   grade your ride
                    road   hilly   dry
                                                    a   b   c   d   e
                    mountain flat   wet
            cross-training   food/water

notes: _____
_____
_____

Thursday

date   time   mileage

average speed   course   grade your ride
                    road   hilly   dry
                                                    a   b   c   d   e
                    mountain flat   wet
            cross-training   food/water

notes: _____
_____
_____

Friday

date	time	mileage

average speed   **course**   **grade your ride**

road   hilly   dry

         a   b   c   d   e

mountain   flat   wet

cross-training   food/water

notes: _____

_____

_____

Saturday

date	time	mileage

average speed   **course**   **grade your ride**

road   hilly   dry

         a   b   c   d   e

mountain   flat   wet

cross-training   food/water

notes: _____

_____

_____

Sunday

date	time	mileage

average speed   **course**   **grade your ride**

road   hilly   dry

         a   b   c   d   e

mountain   flat   wet

cross-training   food/water

notes: _____

_____

_____

Summary

weekly mileage	year to date

notes: _____

_____

_____

_____

Put a knobbier, wider tire on the front wheel of your mountain bike to keep it from sliding out in corners.

TRAINING LOG

Monday

date   time   mileage

average speed   course   grade your ride
                  road   hilly   dry
                                              a   b   c   d   e
                  mountain   flat   wet
          cross-training   food/water

notes: _____
_____
_____

Tuesday

date   time   mileage

average speed   course   grade your ride
                  road   hilly   dry
                                              a   b   c   d   e
                  mountain   flat   wet
          cross-training   food/water

notes: _____
_____
_____

Wednesday

date   time   mileage

average speed   course   grade your ride
                  road   hilly   dry
                                              a   b   c   d   e
                  mountain   flat   wet
          cross-training   food/water

notes: _____
_____
_____

Thursday

date   time   mileage

average speed   course   grade your ride
                  road   hilly   dry
                                              a   b   c   d   e
                  mountain   flat   wet
          cross-training   food/water

notes: _____
_____
_____

Friday

date   time   mileage

average speed   course   grade your ride

road   hilly   dry

mountain   flat   wet

a   b   c   d   e

cross-training   food/water

notes: _____

_____

_____

Saturday

date   time   mileage

average speed   course   grade your ride

road   hilly   dry

mountain   flat   wet

a   b   c   d   e

cross-training   food/water

notes: _____

_____

_____

Sunday

date   time   mileage

average speed   course   grade your ride

road   hilly   dry

mountain   flat   wet

a   b   c   d   e

cross-training   food/water

notes: _____

_____

_____

Summary

weekly mileage   year to date

notes: _____

_____

_____

_____

Wrap tape around your bike's seatpost where it enters the frame, so you can relocate your ideal saddle height if the post slips or is removed.

Monday

date   time   mileage

average speed   course   grade your ride

road   hilly   dry

a   b   c   d   e

mountain   flat   wet

cross-training   food/water

notes: _____
_____
_____

Tuesday

date   time   mileage

average speed   course   grade your ride

road   hilly   dry

a   b   c   d   e

mountain   flat   wet

cross-training   food/water

notes: _____
_____
_____

Wednesday

date   time   mileage

average speed   course   grade your ride

road   hilly   dry

a   b   c   d   e

mountain   flat   wet

cross-training   food/water

notes: _____
_____
_____

Thursday

date   time   mileage

average speed   course   grade your ride

road   hilly   dry

a   b   c   d   e

mountain   flat   wet

cross-training   food/water

notes: _____
_____
_____

Friday

date   time   mileage

average speed   course   grade your ride

road   hilly   dry

       a   b   c   d   e

mountain   flat   wet

cross-training   food/water

notes: _____
_____
_____

Saturday

date   time   mileage

average speed   course   grade your ride

road   hilly   dry

       a   b   c   d   e

mountain   flat   wet

cross-training   food/water

notes: _____
_____
_____

Sunday

date   time   mileage

average speed   course   grade your ride

road   hilly   dry

       a   b   c   d   e

mountain   flat   wet

cross-training   food/water

notes: _____
_____
_____

Summary

weekly mileage   year to date

notes: _____
_____
_____
_____

The farther you ride into the backcountry, the greater your need to ride responsibly. If you become incapacitated, others will have to risk their safety to go in and rescue you.

Monday

date   time   mileage

average speed   course   grade your ride

road   hilly   dry

     a   b   c   d   e

mountain   flat   wet

cross-training   food/water

notes: _____

_____

_____

Tuesday

date   time   mileage

average speed   course   grade your ride

road   hilly   dry

     a   b   c   d   e

mountain   flat   wet

cross-training   food/water

notes: _____

_____

_____

Wednesday

date   time   mileage

average speed   course   grade your ride

road   hilly   dry

     a   b   c   d   e

mountain   flat   wet

cross-training   food/water

notes: _____

_____

_____

Thursday

date   time   mileage

average speed   course   grade your ride

road   hilly   dry

     a   b   c   d   e

mountain   flat   wet

cross-training   food/water

notes: _____

_____

_____

Friday

date   time   mileage

average speed   course   grade your ride

road   hilly   dry

a   b   c   d   e

mountain   flat   wet

cross-training   food/water

notes: _____
_____
_____

Saturday

date   time   mileage

average speed   course   grade your ride

road   hilly   dry

a   b   c   d   e

mountain   flat   wet

cross-training   food/water

notes: _____
_____
_____

Sunday

date   time   mileage

average speed   course   grade your ride

road   hilly   dry

a   b   c   d   e

mountain   flat   wet

cross-training   food/water

notes: _____
_____
_____

Summary

weekly mileage   year to date

notes: _____
_____
_____
_____

Take a cue from fighters who shadowbox to refine technique. Early or late in the day, watch your shadow as you ride, checking for flaws in position, form, and pedaling style.

Monday

date   time   mileage

average speed   course   grade your ride

road   hilly   dry

      a   b   c   d   e

mountain   flat   wet

cross-training   food/water

notes: _____

_____

_____

Tuesday

date   time   mileage

average speed   course   grade your ride

road   hilly   dry

      a   b   c   d   e

mountain   flat   wet

cross-training   food/water

notes: _____

_____

_____

Wednesday

date   time   mileage

average speed   course   grade your ride

road   hilly   dry

      a   b   c   d   e

mountain   flat   wet

cross-training   food/water

notes: _____

_____

_____

Thursday

date   time   mileage

average speed   course   grade your ride

road   hilly   dry

      a   b   c   d   e

mountain   flat   wet

cross-training   food/water

notes: _____

_____

_____

Friday

date   time   mileage

average speed   course   grade your ride

        road   hilly   dry

                                         a   b   c   d   e

        mountain   flat   wet

cross-training   food/water

notes: _____

_____

_____

Saturday

date   time   mileage

average speed   course   grade your ride

        road   hilly   dry

                                         a   b   c   d   e

        mountain   flat   wet

cross-training   food/water

notes: _____

_____

_____

Sunday

date   time   mileage

average speed   course   grade your ride

        road   hilly   dry

                                         a   b   c   d   e

        mountain   flat   wet

cross-training   food/water

notes: _____

_____

_____

Summary

weekly mileage   year to date

notes: _____

_____

_____

_____

Occasionally, take one hand off the handlebar, and shake it vigorously to get the blood flowing and prevent numbness.

Monday

date   time   mileage

average speed   course   grade your ride

road   hilly   dry

a   b   c   d   e

mountain   flat   wet

cross-training   food/water

notes: _____

_____

_____

Tuesday

date   time   mileage

average speed   course   grade your ride

road   hilly   dry

a   b   c   d   e

mountain   flat   wet

cross-training   food/water

notes: _____

_____

_____

Wednesday

date   time   mileage

average speed   course   grade your ride

road   hilly   dry

a   b   c   d   e

mountain   flat   wet

cross-training   food/water

notes: _____

_____

_____

Thursday

date   time   mileage

average speed   course   grade your ride

road   hilly   dry

a   b   c   d   e

mountain   flat   wet

cross-training   food/water

notes: _____

_____

_____

TRAINING LOG

Friday

date   time   mileage

average speed   course   grade your ride

road   hilly   dry

    a   b   c   d   e

mountain   flat   wet

cross-training   food/water

notes: _____
_____
_____

Saturday

date   time   mileage

average speed   course   grade your ride

road   hilly   dry

    a   b   c   d   e

mountain   flat   wet

cross-training   food/water

notes: _____
_____
_____

Sunday

date   time   mileage

average speed   course   grade your ride

road   hilly   dry

    a   b   c   d   e

mountain   flat   wet

cross-training   food/water

notes: _____
_____
_____

Summary

weekly mileage   year to date

notes: _____
_____
_____
_____

The rougher the trail, the more important it is to relax your body and let your bike do its own thing.

Monday

date time mileage

average speed course grade your ride

road hilly dry

   a b c d e

mountain flat wet

cross-training   food/water

notes: _____

_____

_____

Tuesday

date time mileage

average speed course grade your ride

road hilly dry

   a b c d e

mountain flat wet

cross-training   food/water

notes: _____

_____

_____

Wednesday

date time mileage

average speed course grade your ride

road hilly dry

   a b c d e

mountain flat wet

cross-training   food/water

notes: _____

_____

_____

Thursday

date time mileage

average speed course grade your ride

road hilly dry

   a b c d e

mountain flat wet

cross-training   food/water

notes: _____

_____

_____

TRAINING LOG

Friday

date   time   mileage

average speed   course   grade your ride

   road hilly dry   a b c d e

   mountain flat wet

cross-training   food/water

notes: _____
_____
_____

Saturday

date   time   mileage

average speed   course   grade your ride

   road hilly dry   a b c d e

   mountain flat wet

cross-training   food/water

notes: _____
_____
_____

Sunday

date   time   mileage

average speed   course   grade your ride

   road hilly dry   a b c d e

   mountain flat wet

cross-training   food/water

notes: _____
_____
_____

Summary

weekly mileage   year to date

notes: _____
_____
_____
_____

Always put your left foot down when stopping, to prevent chainring "tattoos" on your right leg.

Monday

date   time   mileage

average speed   course   grade your ride

road   hilly   dry

a   b   c   d   e

mountain   flat   wet

cross-training   food/water

notes: _____
_____
_____

Tuesday

date   time   mileage

average speed   course   grade your ride

road   hilly   dry

a   b   c   d   e

mountain   flat   wet

cross-training   food/water

notes: _____
_____
_____

Wednesday

date   time   mileage

average speed   course   grade your ride

road   hilly   dry

a   b   c   d   e

mountain   flat   wet

cross-training   food/water

notes: _____
_____
_____

Thursday

date   time   mileage

average speed   course   grade your ride

road   hilly   dry

a   b   c   d   e

mountain   flat   wet

cross-training   food/water

notes: _____
_____
_____

Friday

	date	time	mileage

average speed   course   grade your ride

road   hilly   dry

a   b   c   d   e

mountain   flat   wet

cross-training   food/water

notes: _____
_____
_____

Saturday

	date	time	mileage

average speed   course   grade your ride

road   hilly   dry

a   b   c   d   e

mountain   flat   wet

cross-training   food/water

notes: _____
_____
_____

Sunday

	date	time	mileage

average speed   course   grade your ride

road   hilly   dry

a   b   c   d   e

mountain   flat   wet

cross-training   food/water

notes: _____
_____
_____

Summary

weekly mileage	year to date

notes: _____
_____
_____
_____

Lighten up on the rear brake if the rear wheel of your mountain bike begins to skid. A turning wheel is more easily controlled than a skidding wheel.

Monday

date time mileage

average speed course grade your ride

road hilly dry

a b c d e

mountain flat wet

cross-training food/water

notes: _____

_____

_____

Tuesday

date time mileage

average speed course grade your ride

road hilly dry

a b c d e

mountain flat wet

cross-training food/water

notes: _____

_____

_____

Wednesday

date time mileage

average speed course grade your ride

road hilly dry

a b c d e

mountain flat wet

cross-training food/water

notes: _____

_____

_____

Thursday

date time mileage

average speed course grade your ride

road hilly dry

a b c d e

mountain flat wet

cross-training food/water

notes: _____

_____

_____

Friday

date   time   mileage

average speed   course   grade your ride

  road hilly dry

           a b c d e

  mountain flat wet

  cross-training   food/water

notes: _____

_____

_____

Saturday

date   time   mileage

average speed   course   grade your ride

  road hilly dry

           a b c d e

  mountain flat wet

  cross-training   food/water

notes: _____

_____

_____

Sunday

date   time   mileage

average speed   course   grade your ride

  road hilly dry

           a b c d e

  mountain flat wet

  cross-training   food/water

notes: _____

_____

_____

Summary

weekly mileage   year to date

notes: _____

_____

_____

_____

Compared to a man of the same height, a woman generally needs a bike that measures about two fewer centimeters between the seat tube and head tube.

Monday

date   time   mileage

average speed   course   grade your ride

road   hilly   dry

          a   b   c   d   e

mountain   flat   wet

cross-training   food/water

notes: _____

_____

_____

Tuesday

date   time   mileage

average speed   course   grade your ride

road   hilly   dry

          a   b   c   d   e

mountain   flat   wet

cross-training   food/water

notes: _____

_____

_____

Wednesday

date   time   mileage

average speed   course   grade your ride

road   hilly   dry

          a   b   c   d   e

mountain   flat   wet

cross-training   food/water

notes: _____

_____

_____

Thursday

date   time   mileage

average speed   course   grade your ride

road   hilly   dry

          a   b   c   d   e

mountain   flat   wet

cross-training   food/water

notes: _____

_____

_____

Friday

date time mileage

average speed   course   grade your ride

    road hilly dry

              a b c d e

    mountain flat wet

cross-training   food/water

notes: _____

_____

_____

Saturday

date time mileage

average speed   course   grade your ride

    road hilly dry

              a b c d e

    mountain flat wet

cross-training   food/water

notes: _____

_____

_____

Sunday

date time mileage

average speed   course   grade your ride

    road hilly dry

              a b c d e

    mountain flat wet

cross-training   food/water

notes: _____

_____

_____

Summary

weekly mileage   year to date

notes: _____

_____

_____

_____

Lower your saddle in winter. If you don't, your position will be too high because of the extra clothing that you'll be sitting on.

Monday

date   time   mileage

average speed   course   grade your ride

  road hilly dry

           a b c d e

  mountain flat wet

cross-training   food/water

notes: _____

_____

_____

Tuesday

date   time   mileage

average speed   course   grade your ride

  road hilly dry

           a b c d e

  mountain flat wet

cross-training   food/water

notes: _____

_____

_____

Wednesday

date   time   mileage

average speed   course   grade your ride

  road hilly dry

           a b c d e

  mountain flat wet

cross-training   food/water

notes: _____

_____

_____

Thursday

date   time   mileage

average speed   course   grade your ride

  road hilly dry

           a b c d e

  mountain flat wet

cross-training   food/water

notes: _____

_____

_____

Friday

date   time   mileage

average speed   course   grade your ride

road   hilly   dry

                        a   b   c   d   e

mountain   flat   wet

cross-training   food/water

notes: _____
_____
_____

Saturday

date   time   mileage

average speed   course   grade your ride

road   hilly   dry

                        a   b   c   d   e

mountain   flat   wet

cross-training   food/water

notes: _____
_____
_____

Sunday

date   time   mileage

average speed   course   grade your ride

road   hilly   dry

                        a   b   c   d   e

mountain   flat   wet

cross-training   food/water

notes: _____
_____
_____

Summary

weekly mileage   year to date

notes: _____
_____
_____
_____

In extremely cold weather, use a cyclocross trick to keep your toes from getting numb: Every half-hour, get off your bike and walk or run for a minute.

Monday

date   time   mileage

average speed   course   grade your ride

road   hilly   dry

a b c d e

mountain   flat   wet

cross-training   food/water

notes: _____

_____

_____

Tuesday

date   time   mileage

average speed   course   grade your ride

road   hilly   dry

a b c d e

mountain   flat   wet

cross-training   food/water

notes: _____

_____

_____

Wednesday

date   time   mileage

average speed   course   grade your ride

road   hilly   dry

a b c d e

mountain   flat   wet

cross-training   food/water

notes: _____

_____

_____

Thursday

date   time   mileage

average speed   course   grade your ride

road   hilly   dry

a b c d e

mountain   flat   wet

cross-training   food/water

notes: _____

_____

_____

Friday

date   time   mileage

average speed   course   grade your ride

road   hilly   dry

      a   b   c   d   e

mountain   flat   wet

cross-training   food/water

notes: _____

_____

_____

Saturday

date   time   mileage

average speed   course   grade your ride

road   hilly   dry

      a   b   c   d   e

mountain   flat   wet

cross-training   food/water

notes: _____

_____

_____

Sunday

date   time   mileage

average speed   course   grade your ride

road   hilly   dry

      a   b   c   d   e

mountain   flat   wet

cross-training   food/water

notes: _____

_____

_____

Summary

weekly mileage   year to date

notes: _____

_____

_____

_____

Carry $5 and some change in your tire repair kit. You can buy a snack on long rides, phone home if you have a breakdown, or pay a driver to drop you off.

WEEKLY MILEAGE

MILEAGE	JAN.	FEB.	MAR.	APR.	MAY	JUN.
☐						
☐						
☐						
☐						
☐						
☐						
☐						
☐						
☐						
WEEKLY TOTAL						
MONTHLY TOTAL						
TOTAL TO DATE						

To chart your weekly mileage, under each month, record the start date of each full training week (for example, January 3, 10, 17, and 24). Estimate your total miles in your most productive week, and divide that number into even increments (for example, 10, 20, 30, 40, 50, 60, 70, 80, 90, and 100 mile increments). Fill in those numbers in the blocks under "Mileage," starting with the lowest number in the block. At

JUL.	AUG.	SEP.	OCT.	NOV.	DEC.	MILEAGE
						WEEKLY TOTAL
						MONTHLY TOTAL
						TOTAL TO DATE

the end of each week, mark the box that corresponds to your total mileage. For example, if you rode 54 miles the week of January 3, in the column for that week, make a mark on the second line in the 50-mile-increment row. As the weeks pass, you'll chart a line graph of your weekly mileage. Keep running totals of your mileage in the "Weekly Total," "Monthly Total," and "Total to Date" blocks at the bottom.

BEST RIDES

date

EQUIPMENT REPAIR

date	bike part	type of repair	upgrade?	price
			☐ yes ☐ no	
			☐ yes ☐ no	
			☐ yes ☐ no	
			☐ yes ☐ no	
			☐ yes ☐ no	
			☐ yes ☐ no	
			☐ yes ☐ no	
			☐ yes ☐ no	
			☐ yes ☐ no	
			☐ yes ☐ no	

RECORD OF INJURIES

date
_____

GEAR CHART FOR 26" WHEELS

These numbers represent "gear inches," which can be used to compare the various combinations of cogs and chainrings. The lower the number, the lower the gear.

Number of teeth on chainring

	24	26	28	30	32	34	36	38	39	40	41	42	43	44	45	46	47	48	49	50	51	52	53	
13	48	52	56	60	64	68	72	76	78	80	82	84	86	88	90	92	94	96	98	100	102	104	106	13
14	45	48	52	56	60	63	67	70	72	74	76	78	80	82	84	85	87	89	91	93	95	97	98	14
15	42	45	49	52	55	59	62	66	68	69	71	73	75	76	78	80	81	83	85	87	88	90	92	15
16	39	42	45	49	52	55	58	61	63	65	67	68	70	72	73	75	76	78	80	81	82	85	86	16
17	37	40	43	46	49	52	55	58	60	61	63	64	66	67	69	70	72	73	75	76	78	80	81	17
18	35	38	40	43	46	49	52	55	56	58	59	61	62	64	65	66	68	69	71	72	74	75	77	18
19	33	36	38	41	44	47	49	52	53	55	565	57	59	60	62	63	64	66	67	68	70	71	73	19
20	31	34	36	39	42	44	47	49	51	52	53	55	56	57	59	60	61	62	64	65	66	68	69	20
21	30	32	35	37	40	42	45	47	48	50	51	52	53	54	56	57	58	59	61	62	63	64	66	21
22	28	31	33	35	38	40	43	45	46	47	48	50	51	52	53	54	56	57	58	59	60	61	63	22
23	27	29	32	34	36	38	41	43	44	45	46	47	49	50	51	52	53	54	55	57	58	59	60	23
24	26	28	30	32	35	37	39	41	42	43	44	45	47	48	49	50	51	52	53	54	55	56	57	24
25	25	27	29	31	33	35	37	39	41	42	43	44	45	46	47	48	49	50	51	52	53	54	55	25
26	24	26	28	30	32	34	36	38	39	40	41	42	43	44	45	46	47	48	49	50	51	52	53	26
27	23	25	27	29	31	33	35	37	38	39	39	40	41	42	43	44	45	46	47	48	49	50	51	27
28	22	24	26	28	30	32	33	35	36	37	38	39	40	41	42	43	44	45	46	46	47	48	49	28
30	21	23	24	26	28	29	31	33	34	35	36	36	37	38	39	40	41	42	43	43	44	45	46	30
32	20	21	23	24	26	28	29	31	32	33	33	34	35	35	37	37	38	39	40	41	41	42	43	32
34	18	20	21	23	24	26	28	29	30	31	31	32	33	34	35	36	37	37	38	38	39	40	41	34
38	16	18	19	21	22	23	25	26	27	27	28	29	29	30	31	31	32	32	33	34	35	36	36	38
	24	26	28	30	32	34	36	38	39	40	41	42	43	44	45	46	47	48	49	50	51	52	53	

Number of teeth on cog

$$\text{Gear inches} = \frac{\text{no. teeth on chainring}}{\text{no. teeth on cog}} \times \text{wheel diameter (inches)}$$

GEAR CHART FOR 27" (700c) WHEELS

	24	26	28	29	30	31	32	33	34	35	36	37	38	39	40	41	42	43	44	45	46	47	48	49	50	51	52	53	54
11	59	64	69	71	74	76	79	81	83	86	88	91	93	96	98	101	103	106	108	110	113	115	118	120	123	125	128	130	133
12	54	59	63	65	68	70	72	74	77	79	81	83	86	88	90	92	95	97	99	101	104	106	108	110	113	115	117	119	122
13	50	54	58	60	62	64	66	69	71	73	75	77	79	81	83	85	87	89	91	93	96	98	100	102	104	106	108	110	112
14	46	50	54	56	58	60	62	64	66	68	69	71	73	75	77	79	81	83	85	87	89	91	93	95	96	98	100	102	104
15	43	47	50	52	54	56	58	59	61	63	65	67	68	70	72	74	76	77	79	81	83	85	86	88	90	92	94	95	97
16	41	44	47	49	51	52	54	56	57	59	61	62	64	66	68	69	71	73	74	76	78	79	81	83	84	86	88	89	91
17	38	41	44	46	48	49	51	52	54	56	57	59	60	62	64	65	67	68	70	71	73	75	76	78	79	81	83	84	86
18	36	39	42	44	45	47	48	50	51	53	54	56	57	59	60	62	63	65	66	68	69	71	72	74	75	77	78	80	81
19	34	37	40	41	43	44	45	47	48	50	51	53	54	55	57	58	60	61	63	64	65	67	68	70	71	72	74	75	77
20	32	35	38	39	41	42	43	45	46	47	49	50	51	53	54	55	57	58	59	61	62	63	65	66	68	69	70	72	73
21	31	33	36	37	39	40	41	42	44	45	46	48	49	50	51	53	54	55	57	58	59	60	62	63	64	66	67	68	69
22	29	32	34	36	37	38	39	41	42	43	44	45	47	48	49	50	52	53	54	55	56	58	59	60	61	63	64	65	66
23	28	31	33	34	35	36	38	39	40	41	42	43	45	46	47	48	49	50	52	53	54	55	56	58	59	60	61	62	63
24	27	29	32	33	34	35	36	37	38	39	41	42	43	44	45	46	47	48	50	51	52	53	54	55	56	57	59	60	61
25	26	28	30	31	32	33	35	36	37	38	39	40	41	42	43	44	45	46	48	49	50	51	52	53	54	55	56	57	58
26	25	27	29	30	31	32	33	34	35	36	37	38	39	41	42	43	44	45	46	47	48	49	50	51	52	53	54	55	56
27	24	26	28	29	30	31	32	33	34	35	36	37	38	39	40	41	42	43	44	45	46	47	48	49	50	51	52	53	54
28	23	25	27	28	29	30	31	32	33	34	35	36	37	38	39	40	41	41	42	43	44	45	46	47	48	49	50	51	52
29	22	24	26	27	28	29	30	31	32	33	34	34	35	36	37	38	39	40	41	42	43	44	45	46	47	47	48	49	50
30	22	23	25	26	27	28	29	30	31	32	32	33	34	35	36	37	38	39	40	41	41	42	43	44	45	46	47	48	49
31	21	23	24	25	26	27	28	29	30	30	31	32	33	34	35	36	37	37	38	39	40	41	42	43	44	44	45	46	47
32	20	22	24	24	25	26	27	28	29	30	30	31	32	33	34	35	35	36	37	38	39	40	41	41	42	43	44	45	46
33	20	21	23	24	25	25	26	27	28	29	29	30	31	32	33	34	34	35	36	37	38	38	39	40	41	42	43	43	44
34	19	21	22	23	24	25	25	26	27	28	29	29	30	31	32	33	33	34	35	36	37	37	38	39	40	41	41	42	43

Number of teeth on chainring

Number of teeth on cog

www.ingramcontent.com/pod-product-compliance
Lightning Source LLC
LaVergne TN
LVHW021448080426
835509LV00018B/2207